CHOICE IN SCHOOLING

CHOICE IN SCHOOLING
A CASE FOR TUITION VOUCHERS
by David W. Kirkpatrick

A Campion Book

Loyola University Press
Chicago

Loyola University Press
3441 N. Ashland Avenue
Chicago, Illinois 60657

Library of Congress Cataloging-in-Publication Data

Kirkpatrick, David W.
 Choice in schooling : a case for tuition vouchers / David W.
Kirkpatrick.
     p. cm.
 Includes bibliographic references (p.) and index.
 ISBN 0-8294-0694-8
 1. Educational vouchers—United States—History.
2. School, Choice of—United States—History. 3. Federal Aid
to education—United States—History. I. Title.
LB2825.K58 1990
379.1'21'0973—dc20   90-40126
                                                                    CIP

To the public school teachers
who know there must be a better way

Contents

Foreword

The decade of the eighties has been tumultuous for American education. Early in this period, we witnessed a torrent of reform reports. In response, some states hiked graduation requirements, curtailed superfluous course offerings, lowered student-teacher ratios, raised teacher salaries, implemented competency tests, restricted extracurricular activities, and boosted overall spending levels significantly. A few states even adopted career ladder schemes and fledgling "alternate certification" programs. Veteran reform watchers could scarcely keep up with the new initiatives.

But as the education reform movement has matured and settled during the latter half of the decade, it has become clear to many of us that these early, "easy" changes tend to produce only incremental improvements in student achievement. Mere tinkering with the same weary delivery system has not failed us, but it has hardly been an unqualified success. Moreover, serious standards-raisers have begun to fear a backlash against the reform movement if the dollars invested therein do not soon produce more palpable improvement.

Accordingly, the focus of the education policy debate has begun to shift away from the course credits, minutes of homework, and "no pass, no play" rules to the more general structural and "cultural" aspects of school organization that help or hinder learning. We are now more apt than before to talk about the design of the school year, the autonomy of teachers, the leadership capabilities of principals, the "ethos" of a school, and educational "professionalism" when we discuss school improvement.

Pundits and educators alike have begun to think more seriously about how parental choice could improve our educational system. Some would say that choice—the notion that families from all socio-economic strata should have a say in selecting the schools, educational programs, or academic courses for their children—is the necessary element for successful school reform.

David Kirkpatrick, whose years in education and government have given him much insight into the multifaceted world of schooling, is properly enthusiastic about choice. And he has now organized this useful resource volume on the voucher system, which is perhaps the best known method of introducing choice into the educational marketplace.

One can make all sorts of theoretical arguments for and against choice in education; this book brims with accumulated wisdom about how choice dovetails neatly with our country's philosophical predilections. But mounting research evidence also supports the notion that choice in education works. One recent study of "public schools of choice" has shown that such schools experience "the breaking down of tight bureaucratic controls" and develop self-renewal strategies, both characteristics of effective schools (and both usually absent from standard public schools). Other research has shown that choice can lead to improved educator professionalism, effective integration, and enhanced student achievement, particularly for students of lower socioeconomic status. In 1986, two Brookings scholars also determined that market place mechanisms (i.e., choice)—not government directives—best lead to these positive changes in school organization and culture.

Choice will be the focus of continuing research projects. The distinguished sociologist James Coleman, for example, is studying what he calls "social capital." His thesis is that one's personal, inner resources—which he or she draws on to succeed in life—are closely related to the strengths and values of the community of which one is part. This community is comprised of one's (extended) family, friends, and the social, religious, economic, and educational institutions he or she encounters regularly. It could well be that the negation of choice in schooling tends to prevent the proper formation of a family's sense of community. If so, this lack of choice may well inhibit the accumulation of a child's social capital.

It is worth noting that choice is something most Americans favor. Poll evidence indicates that the poor and minorities, who generally do not have ready access to educational choice through private schooling or the ability to select their public school districts, are among the most vocal supporters of the voucher concept.

Insofar as this volume contributes to an understanding of the voucher concept as a promising strategy for furthering choice, it will benefit all who read it.

I suspect, however, that the nonincremental increases we seek in educational productivity will not come through choice alone. Further systemic changes must also take place, changes that will reinvigorate elements of the education system shielded from alteration even with a voucher system in place. I'm speaking, of course, about such important reforms as opening up the ranks of teachers and principals to those with experience and expertise in other fields, erecting an accountability system such that educators govern the means of education while legislators determine the outcomes, not vice-versa, compensating crackerjack teachers better than mediocre ones, altering the traditional school year and school day, and making better use of technology. These are changes that could be made without a full-fledged choice system, but they are changes that are apt to be far more powerful with one.

Chester E. Finn, Jr., Director
Educational Excellence Network
Washington, D.C.
and
Former Assistant Secretary
Research and Improvement
U.S. Department of Education

Acknowledgements

Writing may be a lonely occupation, as has been said, but no writer is truly alone. Countless others are present through their influence, if not in person. In some instances this influence may be indirect, the result of having stored impressions from books and articles or been motivated by them. Other influences may be forgotten, or even unknown, the result of some meeting or remark. Still others may have had an impact that was direct and unforgettable.

Among the latter for me was Eupha Bonham, a former Bennington, Vermont, high school English teacher who first suggested education as a career when, during graduation week, she said, "Did you ever think of becoming a teacher?"

Not only was the answer No, but the idea seemed incredible at the time. Fourteen years passed before I entered a high school classroom as the teacher. Yet the incident remains fresh in my mind, as does Eupha Bonham's example of what a teacher can be. That she similarly impressed others was demonstrated by the gathering of many of her former students a few years ago to help her celebrate her 90th birthday, still a very bright and alert lady.

Another such influence has been my wife, Norma. Many a writer gives credit to a spouse for helpful support or criticism. Norma's contribution went far beyond that. Herself a former math teacher, school district department chairperson, and president of the local education association, she is now a computer systems analyst and expert who, in addition to having been there in education and schooling, has been able to bring forth performances from our computer that have been incalculable assistance in the preparation of this work.

1

Introduction

What do Adam Smith, Tom Paine, Thomas Jefferson, John Stuart Mill, Margaret Mead, Milton Friedman, James J. Kilpatrick, former President Ronald Reagan, the 1976 California Supreme Court, former Tennessee Governor Lamar Alexander, Sen. Orrin G. Hatch, President George Bush, and forty-nine percent of the American public (according to a 1988 Gallup poll) have in common?

They have all advocated tuition vouchers, by which support for public education would go to students rather than to institutions. If the individuals named above could all be gathered together in one room today it is possible that this is the only idea upon which they could agree.

An idea that powerful, that enjoys such widespread support, and that has been around for more than two centuries, would seem to have much to recommend it. Yet it has never been generally adopted in basic education. Instead, vouchers have been sometimes condemned as new, radical, untested, or illegal. None of which are correct.

The proposal, though not the name, is literally older than the United States, first appearing in Adam Smith's *Wealth of Nations* in 1776, and even more specifically in Tom Paine's *The Rights of Man* in 1792. So much for new.

As for radical and untried, the Serviceman's Readjustment Act of 1944, commonly known as the GI Bill and generally hailed as the greatest educational innovation in American history, is a tuition voucher, as are the various federal and state student grants in higher education.

Numerous studies and experts have repeatedly suggested that most public funds for general support of higher education be funneled through the students, rather than be given as direct grants to the institutions. While that has yet to be fully implemented, over the years we have moved in that direction.

Even in basic education, as will be shown, the voucher, by various names, has a long and tested history. It is in common practice, for example, in the general student population of some communities in Vermont. It is frequently used across the nation for special-education students who attend private schools at public expense. It has also been estimated by various sources that approximately one-quarter of the funding for private schools in America already comes from public funds, through a mix of programs.

Part of the difficulty, and source of opposition, is the name itself. "Tuition voucher," while descriptive and frequently used, is still a relatively new and strange term to many people. If tuition vouchers were called education grants or student aid, as in higher education, they would be more recognizable, and perhaps less threatening.

Some have tried. A voucher plan has been referred to as a "Baby GI Bill," and as a "Baby BEOG." (Basic Education Opportunity Grants are one form of federal student aid, but apply to higher education despite the words "basic education.") "Educational vouchers" is another variation. Yet no name is as commonly accepted as the practice.

Third-party payments for social services, which is what a tuition voucher is, are very common throughout our society. Suppose, for example, the federal government had used the public school example when Social Security was established in the 1930s. Deciding that financial support for senior citizens was a desirable goal, the government would have levied the necessary taxes to introduce such a plan, as it did, but it would also have established senior citizen homes in which those sixty-five and over would have had to reside in order to receive the program's benefits. Those preferring to live independently would not have received federal funds and would have had to support themselves. While that may sound ridiculous, it is the premise upon which the public school system is based.

Or, consider a more recent program—when it was decided through the political process that some Americans needed aid in order to have sufficient food to eat, the government could have established its own chain of grocery stores, at which those receiving publicly funded groceries would be required to shop. Again, ridiculous. Again, the public school model.

The government school model is also the premise upon which other social services were often at least partially based in the past. There was a time when the penniless were sent to "poor houses" to receive public assistance. Those needing medical services but unable to pay for them had to go to a public, or paupers', hospital. There also have been state homes for veterans, in which elderly veterans resided at public expense rather than receiving assistance permitting them to live independently.

While this approach isn't totally absent today—witness the large public housing projects—the trend has been toward rental assistance grants, Medicare, Medicaid, public assistance allotments, food stamps, and the like.

Public education is the last bastion of compulsory socialism providing social services to the general citizenry. And, like compulsory socialism elsewhere in the world, it doesn't work very well.

A very limited tuition voucher project was conducted in the Alum Rock School District in California for a five-year federally funded project in the 1970s. It was so limited (for example, only public schools in that district could participate and no teachers could lose their jobs) that some question its validity. An interesting feature of this attempt, however, was that the Alum Rock teachers, some of whom belonged to a local affiliate of the National Education Association and some of whom belonged to a local of the American Federation of Teachers, endorsed the project while their national organizations were condemning it.

It was also ironic to see the Representative Assembly of the National Education Association at its 1970 annual meeting in San Francisco adopt a resolution condemning tuition vouchers

even before the project got underway. Aren't educators supposed to teach critical thinking, and problem solving? Why,
then, are they, or their organizations, afraid to think critically to
solve education's problems, or to test a new idea before condemning it? Not only that, many of the thousands of teachers
at that meeting received some of their own education and
training through the GI Bill. In effect, they were unthinkingly
criticizing the practice that helped them further their own
education.

The Reagan Administration proposed that the 98th and
99th Congresses convert the federal program for disadvantaged youngsters to a voucher, which would have given each
recipient about $600. Unable to move such legislation, it was
proposed that the 100th Congress make the vouchers optional
for those local school districts that might wish to utilize them.
And why not? Aside from the use of vouchers for special
education, there are nonoperating public-school districts in the
United States that collect taxes but have no schools, choosing to
send their students to schools in other districts and pay the costs
for educating them there.

As for the legal, or constitutional, question, the U.S. Supreme Court has never ruled that a general voucher system
violates the Constitution's First Amendment separating church
and state. A number of voucher plans have been ruled unconstitutional, but in each instance they were limited to private
schools. These schools are not only overwhelmingly affiliated
with churches, but, as the Court noted, a majority are associated
with just one church.

The California Supreme Court, in *Serrano II*, in 1976,
specifically said the use of tuition vouchers would meet the
court's objection to the then current funding of the state's
public schools.

In a 1983 case from Minnesota, the U.S. Supreme Court
upheld a tuition tax-credit plan which was applied generally.
And, for years, the U.S. Congress and the Supreme Court have
used the voucher concept to provide educational options for
their own pages.

Collectively, it may be deemed both desirable and essential

for a service to be publicly mandated and funded without the government itself providing the service. The worldwide trend is to move more and more social services, including education, toward individual choice rather than government imposition. The best example, perhaps, is Australia. That nation has a provision in its constitution based on, and very similar to, the First Amendment of the U.S. Constitution. It has also moved toward providing more individual choice and control over how education is provided.

In short, the difficulties in initiating or experimenting with a tuition voucher program in the United States are philosophical, political, and practical—given the size and extensiveness of the present public system. They are not legal or constitutional.

They are further complicated because the opposition is well organized and generally united in its stand. Supporters, on the other hand, are neither well organized nor united. Some have indicated support only for their version and extensive or total rejection of some other variation. Many supporters have further damaged their case by stressing their hopes for student and parent control of the schools under a voucher system and the subsequent ability to keep teachers in their "place."

Adam Smith, however, emphasized the negative effect upon teacher status and autonomy of a state-controlled system in which teachers would only be hired hands or civil servants, which has been the case.

The Alum Rock project showed that the role of teachers would be strengthened if they could deal more directly with students and parents. At the same time, the latter would be more pleased because of the element of choice, not control.

This should not be surprising. Laymen do not control any profession, nor is it really likely that they could, since they lack both the intimate knowledge of, and ongoing contact with, details of the profession. But they don't need control, as long as they retain the right to select the professional whose services they will utilize. In this environment, unlike the public schools, no embarrassment is involved in moving from one professional to another because no public notice need be given, nor any reason for the shift. You may change doctors, dentists, lawyers, etc., any time you wish, and no one, including the professional no longer being retained, need know why.

The public schools keep trying to come up with some system of effectively evaluating teachers to retain the good ones and change or remove those deemed unacceptable. No such system has been devised, and probably none ever will be, because of the public nature of such a process. Any effective system of evaluating public employees must, by its very nature, be public and, being public, must necessarily cause embarrassment for those found wanting.

There is no need to go beyond the field of education for evidence of the advantages of choice. Private schools are much smaller, not funded nearly as well and, contrary to the public image and claims of public school personnel, they are not sanctuaries of wealth. In fact, they average about half the per-pupil funding of public schools and have older facilities and fewer resources. Yet, other than the need for funds, the ongoing "crisis" in education which has been with us virtually from the beginning of the public school system does not occur generally in the nonpublic sector.

Private-school teachers, students, and parents all find the environment much more acceptable. The reason is the degree of choice that that system presents to everyone. In contrast, the public school "crisis" not only continues but is worsening, as more and more citizens try to determine for themselves what educational approach their children will experience.

In a mandatory public system, however democratic it tries to be, the majority, or, more frequently, the most powerful minority, determines what will be done. Since unanimity is impossible, even majority rule, if established, always means an unsatisfied minority or minorities. Funding the student rather than the institution will end the "crisis." No centralized approach can, or will, alleviate the spreading and deepening dissatisfaction.

Tuition vouchers are not a panacea. There are even different ideas as to what form a tuition voucher should take. Some have advocated a flat grant, with so many dollars being allocated for each student. Others have said the amount should be variable, with extra compensation for those with extra needs, as is presently the case with expenditures for special-education students, which average about three times those for the typical student. Still others would regulate the vouchers in various ways, such as not allowing any personal money to be added to the sums available through the voucher, or requiring any school receiving vouchers to accept students on a first-come, first-serve basis, using a lottery if there are more applicants than vacancies. Others claim that such restrictions, or many of them at least, are unnecessary, citing the GI Bill and higher-education grants, or vouchers, as examples since these have few such limits or variable compensations.

One final observation. The word "education" is commonly used when it is really more accurate to speak of "schooling," because it is schooling for which the public mandate and control provides, not education. One can be "schooled" without being educated, as was "John Doe," who sued his high school for giving him a diploma despite the fact that he was still illiterate (he lost the case). One can also be educated without being schooled, as were John Stuart Mill and Theodore Roosevelt, and, in our time, Margaret Mead. It is schooling which is being criticized, not education.

2

The Perceived Need for Change

There would be no discussion of tuition vouchers, tuition tax credits, alternative education, private schools, or other changes in or from the present public school system if that system were not so consistently, so seriously, so widely, and so compellingly found wanting. From Edmund Burke to Alvin Toffler, and through innumerable studies of public schooling in the aggregate or particular, the public schools have been subject to constant criticism, criticism amply justified by the evidence.

Some of today's critics are fond of referring to the good old days in education, days that never existed. For example, much is made today of the loss of respect for teachers, how they once were regarded with high esteem and status. Such as Ichabod Crane?—the teacher in Washington Irving's *The Legend of Sleepy Hollow*.

How few remember the days, even in this century, when some teachers worked for room and board; when some lived in "teacherages"; when smoking, drinking, or the marriage of a woman teacher was cause for immediate dismissal; when teachers were permitted one night a week for "courting" if permission was received in advance. As poorly paid and respected as they may think they now are, today's public school teachers are an aristocracy compared with their predecessors.

Concern is expressed today because teachers tend to come from the lower ranks of college students. While this has been recently aggravated because capable women have more career options today, the general proposition was as true twenty, thirty, or more years ago as it is today. Teachers have been consistently drawn disproportionately from the lower academic ranks.

As for achievement, former Labor Secretary William Brock said 700,000 high school graduates annually are functional illiterates. As unacceptable as that may be, at the turn of the century only six percent of the high school age group got as far as high school.

Volumes have been written on the problems of both public and private schooling, but of public schools in particular. Some, like the works of Jonathan Kozol, are very bitter and charge a conspiracy to keep ordinary pupils, as well as minorities, in their "place." Perhaps.

More likely, however, is the charge of Charles Silberman that the real problem with the schools is their "mindlessness." Few really know what they are doing, or have the time or interest to consider what might be. Educators, as a group, are not great readers. One study in 1967 of Indiana history teachers indicated that the average teacher surveyed read less than one book per year pertaining to his or her field. Later surveys have not altered the impression that teachers are seldom scholars.

It is also true that there never has been a genuine teacher shortage, even in schooling's growth years of the 1960s. What there was, and what there may be again in the near future, was a shortage of teachers in the classroom, which isn't the same thing as a teacher shortage. There are more qualified, or at least certified, teachers in society at large, pursuing other careers and interests, than are needed in classrooms.

A number of surveys over the years have indicated that the average teacher stays in that role only five to ten years, and that low salaries are usually not the prime reason for their departure (although some recent surveys have money higher on the list than in the past; which is ironic because salaries, in constant dollars, are higher now, than they used to be). For example:

> Interviews with ex-teachers across the country, who
> freely discussed why they quit, brought a startling

chorus of blame addressed to The System. By the teachers' definition, The System consists of: (1) know-nothing school boards, (2) insecure, inadequate principals, (3) doting parents, (4) rebellious or apathetic children, and (5) poorly trained teachers drawn from the bottom of the college-educated group . . . The average continuous teaching career in U.S. public schools lasts only five years. (Richard Meryman in *Student, School and Society*, ed. John A. Dahl et al., 1964)

Major reasons for teachers leaving the classroom continue to be dissatisfaction with the present system, complaints about the inordinate amount of paperwork, the constant interruptions, the lack of adequate support or respect, and the inability to do the job as the teacher thinks it should be done—in short, the inability to function as a professional.

Few occupations stress the word "professional" as much as do teachers and their organizations; yet, at heart, teachers know that they are not professionals, that they are not regarded as such. This is partially because too few are willing to conduct themselves as professionals, though many teachers might make the counterclaim that they are not permitted to do so.

The term "professional" is not carefully defined in general usage. You can hear workers of many classifications describe themselves as professionals after they have been involved in the same occupation over a long period of time.

A bit more technically, a professional is one who has a considerable degree of autonomy and control of his or her working conditions and procedures. A professional is also one who works with a patient, client, or customer on a mutually voluntary basis.

Public school teachers do not meet this standard. Nor, apparently, do they wish to do so. While they argue for professionalism, self-determination, the right to establish the standards for the "profession," and the like, many are equally quick to oppose any loosening of the restrictions on pupils and parents to allow them an equal share of self-determination.

This is not restricted to opposing tuition vouchers. The

opposition is equally strong to any suggestions for open enrollment, in which students could decide what school they will attend or what teacher they will have. A wide variety of arguments are presented why this is not a good idea, or why it is an impossible one, but the fact remains that those who insist on a captive clientele, possessing few or no options concerning that to which they are exposed, will of necessity continue to be regarded as prison guards. For that is what they are, several hours a day, approximately 180 days a year.

This position creates an unending cycle. Teachers who object to the present arrangement, with some noteworthy exceptions, sooner or later opt out of the system because they can no longer tolerate the coercion it entails—coercion by them as well as coercion of them.

The standard answers to the present system's faults are no answers at all. Worse than no answers, they have been tried and they have failed. Almost tragically, incomprehensibly, there are those who have seen the proposed answers tried, seen them fail, and yet continue to advocate them.

A generation ago John Henry Martin put the platitudes to the test and found them wanting. The things that are supposed to make public schools work were tried: more money; more teachers, which would result in smaller classes; more specialists. And they didn't work. Martin realized they didn't work, wrote that they didn't work, and admitted that the emperor had no clothes. But these same ideas continue to be promoted and believed.

Martin was the superintendent of a school district which supported an increase in the budget of thirty-five percent, making possible many changes that are supposed to make for efficient schools and effective education.

Average class size went from over thirty pupils to about twenty. Specialists of all kinds were hired or increased in number: guidance counselors, psychologists, social workers, classroom aides, and remedial teachers. Two full-time remedial reading teachers were assigned to each elementary school in which the average enrollment was six hundred students.

Teachers with advanced degrees were hired, the curriculum was updated, an extensive in-service program for teachers was initiated, a teacher council was chosen by secret ballot, and dozens of other reforms were introduced.

After two years, outside evaluators were hired to make a thorough and detailed assessment of the results.

Students took achievement tests, with the results analyzed by class size, teacher age and experience, and the students' race, sex, and family income.

Martin reported:

> In the end, the cherished faith died . . . all that was done to make a difference had made no difference. The panaceas were, after all, only false promises—vain expectations. All the patented prescriptions . . . that made such a grand appearance in the college textbooks and the theses of the pedagogues had failed the hard test of reality in the field. (Martin and Harrison 1972, 1-3)

In 1970, a few years prior to the appearance of Martin's book but after the effort that he described, similar testimony came from Neil Sullivan, former superintendent of schools in Berkeley, California.

Sullivan told a Senate committee that his district had also lowered class size, provided remedial teachers, and the like, only to conclude three years later that inner city children not only did not gain thereby but had actually lost ground (Kilpatrick, Nov. 23, 1970, 2).

Perhaps the most extensive example was New York City's More Effective Schools Program, initiated and supported by the New York local of the American Federation of Teachers, and implemented by school district authorities. This program was carried on in selected schools for a number of years with results similar to those detailed by Martin and Sullivan, but never similarly publicly acknowledged.

MES should have more properly been termed the More Expensive Schools Program, because that was its main accomplishment. It succeeded in spending considerably greater sums of money, but not in gaining added academic achievement by the students. It was also evaluated and found wanting, despite smaller classes (a teacher-pupil ratio of less than one to twelve), more experienced teachers, greater per-pupil expenditures, better facilities, compensatory education efforts, and all the rest. Of twenty-one schools, only four had students who read at grade level on average, and these schools contained mostly middle-class white students. The background of the students again appeared far more important than anything the schools were doing (Pa. State Education Assn., April 6, 1970).

When the New York City fiscal crisis developed in the mid-seventies, the MES program was discontinued, with minimum fanfare. The irony is that both the Federation and the National Education Association, to which most of the nation's teachers belong, continue to advocate the same techniques. They neither suggest, encourage, nor accept any alternatives that do not fit into the conventional methodology and operations with which they are already familiar. Worse, they strenuously object to even pilot projects or research efforts that might arrive at contrary conclusions. Apparently, they are willing to try any change as long as it doesn't alter the basic structure of public schooling. Their public pronouncements would lead one to believe that more money, more teachers, more this, and more that are all that is needed to provide effective education, and imply that these are established facts that only await implementation. If only it were so.

Not that money isn't required, or that teachers shouldn't receive decent salaries, or that some classes may not be too big. But these things, by themselves, cannot and will not do the job, and this has been frequently demonstrated for anyone willing to look.

Those wishing to review this further, at greater depth, should read works by Bestor (1953), Conant (1961), Kozol (1967), Silberman (1970), Hentoff (1977), The National Commission on Excellence (1983), Goodlad (1984) or Brimelow (1986), to name just a few.

If professionals from various fields who died at the turn of the century could be brought back and returned to their prior positions, the teachers would have the easiest time adjusting. Oh, they would find some changes. Schools are bigger. They would have to make some technical adjustments—to movie projectors, fancier textbooks, even computers. But, for all the talk of change, for all the studies, all the research, all the reformers, all the outside changes, and all the pressure for educational change, the essential process remains the same: one teacher and a group of students together in a box with the teacher talking most of the time, that is, in a teacher-centered situation where the teacher talks more than all of the students combined. There are, of course, exceptions, but they are just that—exceptions—and most of them still conform to the basic setup. Of course, there are instances where a caring, sensitive and creative teacher makes it a point not to be so dominant.

Needed change apparently cannot, and will not, be brought about by those currently in the field, however much they like to talk of change, reform, or even revolution. Professions, like other "establishments," are rarely changed from within.

Experts are experts of the status quo, of what is rather than what can be or what should be. They benefit from the established way of doing things, or think they do, and they don't want to risk losing what they have, for promises of a better way. The future has no constituency. The status quo does, which is why it is the status quo.

The Flexner Report, which transformed the medical profession early in this century, was not produced by a medical professional. The leading names in education, from Jean Jacques Rousseau to John Dewey to Christopher Jencks, have rarely been education majors or public school educators. They have been economists, sociologists, and anthropologists.

If the public waits until the "professionals" change the system, it will never happen. The evidence is centuries old. Edmund Burke in the eighteenth century, Ralph Waldo Emerson in the nineteenth, and George Bernard Shaw in the twentieth are but a few examples of noted critics of schooling. They held that more learning occurs outside of a classroom than within; that, after years of schooling, we emerge and "do not know a thing"; and that school is a horrible experience, worse than a prison.

> The range of criticism, the persistent efforts to reform education from the early nineteenth century on, suggest that Americans have never been satisfied with their schools. (Lazerson et al., 1985, 111)

Most people, if questioned closely, are really not happy with their schooling experience. Better than twenty-five percent of students still do not complete high school. Most who remain do so because of necessity and lack of options. Those who express some satisfaction with schooling, upon inquiry, generally do so because of their friends, because of extracurricular activity, or for other reasons having little or nothing to do with the academic teacher-learner process for which the schools were created.

Perhaps most tragic of all are those who remain within the system to little avail. They are the hundreds of thousands who finish high school or, in some publicized cases involving athletes, spend several years in college and remain functional illiterates.

While everything human is subject to imperfection, error, and problems, is there any other system in society which continues to be tolerated despite such an unending high percentage of dissatisfaction and outright failure?

To raise these issues, to see the emperor unclothed, is often to become the subject of not merely rebuttal but vitriolic attack. As Josiah Gilbert Holland said years ago:

> We Americans make a God of our common-school system. It is treason to speak a word against it. A man is regarded as a foe to education who expresses any doubt of the value of it. But. . . it is a hindrance and a failure. (Kerber 1968, 208)

LIFE magazine, in a 1958 series of articles on education, thought it saw some improvement:

> For years most critics of U.S. education have suffered the curse of Cassandra—always to tell the truth, seldom to be listened to or believed. But now the curse has been lifted. What they were saying is beginning to be believed. The schools are in terrible shape.

The passage of years has shown that the critics were not believed and the schools are still in terrible shape. The principle difference now is that, as is so often true, many have forgotten history and look upon the 1950s as among "the good old days" of education.

As Paul Goodman wrote: "Apparently the schooling that we have already had has brainwashed everybody" (Goodman 1964, 148).

Colin Greer has summarized this unhappy history of schooling from before the turn of the century.

> From 1890, at least, the schools failed to perform according to their own as well as the popular definition of their role. In virtually every study undertaken since that of Chicago schools made in 1898, more children have failed in school than have succeeded, both in absolute and in relative numbers. (Greer 1969)

He also notes the common belief that the schools had some "golden past" that has been lost. While comforting to many, this belief is also harmful in that it can lead to the conclusion that all we need do is return schooling to the magic age and all will be well. Like Jonathan Kozol and others, Greer says not only is this not true, and a vain hope, but that public education has never served youngsters of lower social standing and, in fact, was never intended to do so. Our present problems, therefore, do not occur because schools have changed, but rather because they have not changed and still do what they have always done.

During my term as president of the Pennsylvania State Education Association that had then more than 100,000 members, I presented the following opinion in the *Pennsylvania School Journal:*

> Educators must cease supporting a facade of quality where the substance is missing. Our schools have never approached the effectiveness they should have, and they do not approach it now. We need not hide that fact, nor be apologetic for it, since we have not been responsible for it.

> It wasn't noticed years earlier because it did not matter until just recently. The blacks, the Indians, the poor of

whatever color, the first generation immigrant, and others who were politically impotent, have always received rather short shrift from our educational system, public and private. (Kirkpatrick, May 1970, 234)

It is important for public-school educators, especially the teachers, to keep in mind that much of the criticism over the years is not directed at them personally, and certainly not at the need for an educated citizenry. The criticism of the system is just that: criticism of the system. Much of it is generated, not by a lack of faith in education but by the exact opposite, by a strong faith in the importance of every child and every citizen acquiring a good education.

And it is this, an educated citizenry, in which all of us, as expressed collectively through the instrument of government, have an interest. How that education is achieved, through what instrument and by what pedagogical process, should not be the prime concern of government.

Government essentially coerces parents to send their children to a government mandated, funded, owned, operated, and regulated institution. It is not name-calling to describe this practice as socialism. It is true that those who can afford an alternative can escape this coercion, but even that was made possible only by a U.S. Supreme Court ruling.

Oregon attempted to require all students to attend public schools. The 1925 Court, in *Pierce v. Society of Sisters*, said this was unconstitutional.

If every family had enough money, the parents could educate their children as desired, as long as they were educated. The Court in 1925 did not rule that the government could not mandate that its citizens be educated. To the contrary, it held that education was a desirable goal, but that families have wide latitude as to how that goal was achieved. The "catch" is that families need the funds to exercise that option.

Funding education through the student, rather than through the institution, would enable every family to enjoy the constitutional protection now only available to those with sufficient financial resources.

Unless and until that is so, as Peter Schrag said,

a system that requires all children (except the very rich who can buy their way out) to attend a particular school for a specified period . . . must be judged by its failures. (Schrag 1970)

As long as public educators are provided a clientele by coercion, they must be prepared for the harsh criticism of Schrag and others for "the boredom, the emptiness, the brutality, the stupidity, the sheer waste of the average classroom" (Schrag 1970).

There are, of course, options available to the public schools short of funding through tuition vouchers. Open enrollment, with students permitted to attend the school of their choice on a space-available basis, is a possibility and a growing reality. This could be carried further, with students permitted to choose their teachers, and teachers allowed to do the same with students. Other professions have such mutual choice, why should the schools not do the same, even if it requires changing some laws? Of course, that could create problems for a teacher, or a student, that no one selected. In the unlikely event this occurred, and it rarely does in other professions, it would certainly send that person a message.

Such flexibility, among other options, works in other fields. There is no reason to believe it would not work in education as well, despite the claims of educators to the contrary.

Ewald Nyquist has noted some of schooling's abundant myths: that one only learns while young and attending an institution in an unbroken sequence of many years duration; that knowledge may only be acquired from a teacher; that one is educated only if proper credits and credentials are acquired; that segregation by age is necessary; that academic achievement is paramount and other talents are, at best, minor; and that only the "schooled" are deserving of merit.

It is Ian Lister's opinion that schools use their failure to teach as the basis for requesting additional funds to correct the situation.

According to an educational law of eventually diminishing returns, increased investment leads to increased failure and, in its turn, to arguments for yet more investment. This creates an exponential increase in the cost of failure. A developed country is one that can afford failure at the highest per capita cost. (Lister 1974, 4)

Those who are shocked by the idea of alternatives to the present system of schooling need to be reminded that the present system had its origins only two centuries ago, did not become reasonably well established until the middle of the last century, and only became common for great numbers of youngsters in this century.

Our system of schooling evolved in the nineteenth century, largely based upon a model originating under both Prussian and Napoleonic interests. It is of more than casual relevance that these were essentially authoritarian regimes and, in later years, especially in Bismarck's Prussia, there was no mistaking the purpose of state-run schools: to indoctrinate the next generation and bring about an orderly society of obedient citizens.

This remains a major purpose of schooling around the world, although often in a less self-conscious manner. The system is so familiar today that its origins are generally unknown and lost in the mists of history. So it is easy to speak of "good citizenship" as a goal of the schools without clearly understanding and defining what we mean in a supposedly democratic society—in contrast to what the same term means in an openly autocratic system.

In 1524 Martin Luther called for compulsory public schools, arguing that it would better prepare young men for military service and instruct them in their religion. This would give the state a greater war potential at the same time it suppressed religious dissent.

During the same century compulsory schools were established in Geneva by John Calvin, another religious reformer, with similar objectives. Holland, influenced by Calvin, established compulsory public schools in the early 1600s. The Puritans who created the Massachusetts Bay Colony were Calvinists from Holland and they brought compulsory schooling with them.

As compulsory schooling became more common it helped foster the theory that, at least as far as education was concerned, children belong to the government and not to their parents (Lytle 1975, 54-55).

If it is essential to have government schools to have an educated populace, good citizens, and the like, there should be some demonstrable evidence that graduates of these schools are better educated, better citizens, more likely to vote, more tolerant towards others, etc., than are graduates of the private schools. No such evidence exists. Private school alumni are not distinguishable in society from former public school students. There is even some evidence that graduates of Catholic parochial schools are more tolerant than Catholic graduates of public schools.

If this is so, the need for state-run schools is considerably weakened. In any event, the burden of proof should be upon those who opt for educational coercion.

The Pierce case has already been mentioned. In 1976, the Supreme Court of Vermont cited that decision as the basis for rejecting criminal actions against parents who were sending their children to non-approved schools. It might be noted here that Vermont is a state where tuition vouchers for basic education have been used for many years.

The U.S. Supreme Court itself, in *Wisconsin v. Yoder*, in 1972, held that, in at least some circumstances, "compulsory attendance, even in an equivalency basis, must yield to First Amendment concerns."

In terms of specific practices, groups of students moving together from year to year originated in Germany; and the concept of one pupil to a desk arose in England in the nineteenth century, however universal it may be today. There was more variety in the early days, with classes sometimes containing hundreds of students—something virtually unheard of today. Peer teaching was a common, and effective, technique.

This latter practice has been an almost unqualified success wherever it has been used, one of the more interesting applications coming when "slow" sixth-grade students were assigned to assist regular first-graders. The assumption was that this would be helpful for the younger students. It was. But the most interesting development was the relative blossoming of the sixth graders. For many of them it came as a delightful surprise to discover that they weren't as "stupid" as they had come to believe; that they did, in fact, know something which they could successfully transmit to others.

Despite this, schools generally seek to preserve the "rights" of the professionals and the impression that there is some mystique to teaching that only the properly initiated can understand. This also increases the need for teachers in greater numbers, with a corresponding increase in the cost of the schooling provided.

This mystique has considerably weakened over the years. In an age when virtually everyone is exposed to schooling, and individuals are therefore in a position to decide what worth it may have, it is increasingly difficult to maintain the fiction that schooling is all its defenders claim it to be.

There are increasing numbers of people who believe that much of what the present system involves is useless at best, and harmful at its worst.

Psychologist Robert Gagne and measurement expert Gene Glass, among others, question whether traditional high school education serves a useful purpose for the majority or whether the schools accomplish anything toward achieving the goals of helping children to develop emotional maturity and other desirable social characteristics (Gowin 1981, 9-10).

Study after study confirms the ineffectiveness and the waste. For example, studies by researchers at the University of Pennsylvania, the Rand Corporation, and elsewhere question the effect of the fifty billion dollars spent on Chapter I programs in its first twenty years. Indications are that more money went to non-poor than to poor students and to average students rather than those needing remedial work. There is also disagreement over whether there have been long-term gains (Kelley 1986).

In at least one instance, in a southwestern state, the funds didn't even go to the non-poor or average students; it was discovered that they were used to put wall-to-wall carpeting and a color television set in the school district's central administrative offices.

The perceived need for change is widespread. For example:

Alvin Toffler has written that a school system which simulates factory life is obsolete. It is producing workers for factories that won't be there. As a result, we're in deep trouble (Toffler 1986, 48).

According to Xerox CEO David T. Kearns "Public education is the most hierarchical institution we have left in this country" (Kearns 1986, 566).

A study of 11,000 educators at 400 public and private high schools, by John E. Chubb, a senior fellow at the Brookings Institution in Washington, and Terry Moe of Stanford University, concluded that private-school teachers and principals, knew more about their jobs and liked them better than did public school staff. These findings complement data from the U.S. Department of Education that private school students are better achievers.

Public teachers are demoralized by the bureaucracy, said Chubb, and any attempted reform of the public schools will fail unless they learn from the experience and practice of private institutions. This means control of public schools should be transferred to the parents, teachers and principals of those schools. This could be done, say the researchers, if parents could choose the schools their children attend and if school funding was enrollment based (Painter 1986).

Let's pursue that idea.

3

1776-1954
Evolution of an Idea

The 1776 to 1954 era was, at best, embryonic for tuition vouchers in the United States. Although the idea first appeared in two classics of British and American literature—Adam Smith's *Wealth of Nations* and Tom Paine's *The Rights of Man*—as well as Thomas Jefferson's school bill for Virginia in 1779, it received little attention during this period. This is perhaps partially because neither work, although frequently referred to and quoted, is regarded as a treatise on education. Smith's text is a foundation piece of laissez-faire economics and Paine's is a political document.

Smith's comments are concerned largely with the effect on teachers of being public employees rather than educational entrepreneurs. Although he was writing in the eighteenth century, and more concerned with higher education than elementary or secondary education, anyone who has spent much time as a public school teacher will recognize Smith's description of what happens when funds go to institutions rather than to individuals.

While relatively little was being said during this period that directly concerned tuition vouchers, there were important developments establishing the groundwork for present-day legal interpretations.

As early as 1907, the U.S. Supreme Court upheld a

requirement that a public transit company provide half-price transportation to students. The next year it ruled that Indians could use funds for their children to attend parochial schools, even though those funds were in the care of the federal government. This was a specialized instance, the Court holding that these monies were really private, the property of the Indian tribes. The right of Native First Americans to have educational choice was thus affirmed. The most severe test of this right came from Oregon in the early 1920s, and it involved an attempt by the general citizenry to terminate it.

In 1922, by public initiative, Oregon established that all students must attend public schools. On June 1, 1925, the U.S. Supreme Court ruled that this was unconstitutional. Associate Justice James Clark McReynolds, speaking for the Court, said, "The child is not the mere creature of the state," and that parents have a right to determine the manner of their children's education. Possessing a right and being able to practice it are not interchangeable propositions, as growing numbers of Americans realize.

In a 1927 Louisiana case, the Court said a state could not unreasonably regulate private schools, by determining such things as textbook content and teacher qualifications. Speaking for the Court, Justice McReynolds said this could destroy private schools and "deprive parents of fair opportunity to procure for their children instruction which they think important."

In 1930, on a positive note, the Court held constitutional a Louisiana law providing free textbooks for students in public and private schools, holding that it was the students who benefited, not the institutions.

This is a consistent position the Court has taken over the years regarding school aid. Where such assistance was generally applied the Court upheld it. Any effect on nonpublic schools, even parochial schools, has been viewed as incidental and not a violation of the First Amendment or the separation of church and state.

One of the Court's most dramatic and controversial school rulings came in 1943, when it overturned a West Virginia provision compelling students to salute the flag and pledge allegiance to it. To many people, then and since, saluting the flag seemed a modest indication of national loyalty and objections to it demonstrated a weakening of the national moral fiber.

In one of the more powerful statements regarding individual rights, Associate Justice Robert H. Jackson wrote: "The Fourteenth Amendment protects the citizen against the State itself and all of its creatures—Boards of Education not excepted." He expressed concern over attempting to mold public opinion into one model.

In words that almost predicted the current struggle over schools, he said:

> As governmental pressure toward unity becomes greater, so strife becomes more bitter as to whose unity it will be. Probably no deeper division of our people could proceed from any provocation than from finding it necessary to choose what doctrine and whose program public educational officials shall compel youth to unite in embracing. Ultimate futility of such attempts to compel coherence is the lesson of every such effort . . . we apply the limitation of the Constitution with no fear that freedom to be intellectually and spiritually diverse or even contrary will disintegrate the social organization.

Unfortunately, a great many citizens do not share Jackson's confidence in such diversity. Strangely, one of the major sources of opposition to tuition vouchers, or family control of children's education, has come from liberals, who normally claim to be strong advocates of individual freedoms. In this instance, however, they express strong support for the public school system because deviations from it would weaken "social cohesion"—a dogmatic claim generally made with no supporting evidence.

Ignore for the moment whether the school system has been responsible for such cohesion, especially as distinct from that provided by nonpublic schools, and whether, even if it did in the past, it has such a role today. Put aside consideration of the extreme mobility of the population and of the influence movies, television, and other means of cultural transmission to which children are today exposed. Such a view still demonstrates a lack of faith in democracy and a pluralistic society, two themes given much lip service.

In the words of Justice Jackson:

> freedom to differ is not limited to things that do not matter much. That would be a mere shadow of freedom. The test of its substance is the right to differ as to things that touch the heart of the existing order.

It is a test that too many fail.

One need not agree that the presence of *The Wizard of Oz* in the classroom is a threat to a child's moral standards because of a reference to a "wicked witch," as was argued in a 1986 court case, in order to accept the right of parents to hold that belief and wish to have their child attend a school more in accord with their wishes and values.

That, indeed, as Justice Jackson noted, is the test of a belief in democracy and freedom of speech and thought. Are we prepared to grant that freedom only to those who think as we do, or shall it be granted to everyone?

It needs to be recalled that for most of our history there was no public school system. It began to emerge 150 years ago, and compulsory attendance was extensively established only at the end of the nineteenth century.

Most citizens prior to that time—including the Founding Fathers responsible for the creation of the nation and the writing of its constitution—were educated either at home, in nonpublic schools, or by a tutor. There is even evidence that literacy was higher in the nineteenth century than today.

Finally, those who care not for historical allusions but only for today still have the burden to prove that students in nonpublic schools are less well educated or poorer citizens. Lacking such proof, there is no justification for educational coercion on behalf of public schooling.

There is another important significance to be grasped about court cases having to do with public schooling. Those who think that the *Brown v. Board of Education* desegregation decision of 1954 was an aberration by the court do not know the history of events that led up to it. For decades the NAACP had pursued one court case after another, establishing the rights of minorities in one way here, in another way there, building a foundation of precedents for the culminating decision affecting schools nationwide.

The same process may be taking place regarding the educational rights of students and parents, although less consciously since no single organization or group is coordinating the effort. Nevertheless, a body of cases that protect these rights is being built, and many of them are cited in this work.

Pierce alone made clear the fundamental right of parents to decide what form of education they wished for their child. It did not, however, indicate any right to public funding for that end. That day may or may not arrive.

What has gradually emerged is the legality of such aid, whether or not it is a "right." Nonpublic-school parents have been protected against undue interference by the government in how they may educate their children, and may now receive aid for textbooks, transportation, and many other services.

In a 1983 case, *Mueller v. Allen,* the U.S. Supreme Court upheld general aid, in this instance in the form of tuition tax credits, for all students and their parents. Since a tuition voucher is even more broadly based, going as well to those whose income is too low for them to pay taxes, it seems that such a case would also be constitutionally acceptable.

Additional proof is the GI Bill. Since 1944, millions of Americans have received educational aid, which not only covered school costs but granted supplemental subsistence funding as well. Those utilizing the GI Bill attended public and private institutions, including proprietary or profit-making schools, as well as seminaries and other religious schools when they studied to become members of the clergy.

Everyone was eligible, and they could use the aid at any institution which met federal approval, a very wide range. The only requirement was that the individual had to have some stated minimum period of military service.

Why restrict this concept to veterans? Does this not discriminate against those who do not, or are unable to, perform military service? From a public policy point of view, should not a program of such outstanding success, value, and constitutionality be extended to the general citizenry? This returns us to the issue of the growing number of precedents regarding education and individual choice.

Stephen Arons's *Compelling Belief* (1983) presents the provocative argument that separation of school and state is even more important than separation of church and state. A coordinated effort to tie together court decisions over the years conceivably could lead to this result.

The argument in favor of such a decision is both philosophical and legal. Millions of Americans belong to no church at all. Other millions belong only on a nominal or occasional basis. Even active churchgoers may average only a few hours a week in religious or church-related activity. Furthermore, there are hundreds of denominations from which to choose, and a person may move from one to another with relative ease. This is a result of the fundamental right of religious freedom in our society, which includes the right to refrain as well as to participate.

Given that argument, should not the right of educational freedom be even more fundamental?

For one thing, we have long since decided as a society that education is not optional. Everyone should be educated. Furthermore, education is not an incidental or casual experience. Typically, a student attends school for five to five and one- half instructional hours a day, for 180 days a year, or nearly a thousand hours annually, for twelve years. This does not include the additional hours the student may be subject to the school's control—for home room, study halls, lunch periods, extracurricular activities, and the like.

Clearly the impact of thousands of hours of schooling can be much more compelling than the impact of a church, yet parents do not have many variations in schooling from which to choose. In fact, some choices that exist are not available to millions of Americans who do not have either sufficient funds, after taxes, to pay for nonpublic schooling or the affluence to move into one of the wealthy communities, where a school might satisfy their needs.

A wealthy community can afford to spend much more than the average amount on their schools, and can write part of that off against their income, since, unlike rent, property taxes (the main source of local support for schools) and interest on a mortgage are deductible from income subject to the federal income tax—deductions not available to the poor and renters. Furthermore, the wealthier the individual or family, the greater the size of this tax break (or educational subsidy—which is what it really is in such cases). The use of vouchers would make such subsidies not only apparent but more fairly distributed among the populace at large. How the precedents are leading in this direction will be developed in both this and subsequent chapters.

Although the ultimate destination is yet unknown, the journey we are on began with Adam Smith, Thomas Jefferson, and Tom Paine.

The Wealth of Nations, generally regarded as an economic text, has in Book II an extensive section on education that includes many psychological insights (predating the modern professional psychologists), which two centuries later read like predictions.

One of these was Smith's observation that those paid from the public purse, including teachers, lack the motivation for performance possessed by those in the private realm. This is not due to any lack of moral fiber on the part of the former relative to the latter, but because of the different circumstances in which they find themselves. He therefore held that private individuals should pay at least some of the costs for teachers but that government should aid those who would be unable to take care of these costs from their own means.

Smith said private funding is needed because, in every occupation, most individuals exert effort in their work only to the degree they must, and this necessity is greatest for those who need to attract their sources of income. If the state is the source, with income received without regard to individual effort, exertions will be minimized. He extended this argument to include school and college endowments that permit paying teacher salaries "independent of their success and reputation in their particular professions."

Smith regarded it as in the individual's interest to live as easily as possible. If his income is the same regardless of effort, it is in his interest to do as little as possible. Realizing that many individuals are by nature energetic, he still held that it would be in their interest to use this energy in supplemental activity "from which he can derive some advantage, rather than in the performance of his duty, from which he can derive none."

Not only that, such teachers will mutually support the inattention to duty by others, in return for which they may neglect their own. He used as an example the Oxford of his day where, he said, most of the professors had for many years stopped even pretending to teach.

He noted that all public authorities can do is force the teacher to have some number of pupils for a certain amount of hours and give so many lectures (or classes, in today's system) each week or year. The quality of those lectures, or that performance, is still dependent upon the teacher.

Today's laws for public schools generally require five to five and one-half hours of daily instruction. A teacher is assigned so many classes per day, with so many students per class—assignments generally independent of the wishes of either the teacher or the students. The subject matter of the classes may be determined, but there is a wide variation in the quality of individual teachers' performances. This is not a matter subject to state control, except in the very broadest sense, but by the teacher's attitudes and skills, variations of which have little or no bearing on the teacher's salary. True, salaries generally vary according to degrees attained and years of experience, but neither of these factors has given proof of having any but the most modest impact on the quality of teaching. Some research even suggests that their impact is negative.

For example, one study years ago concluded that teacher performance improves during the first five years, and then levels off or declines. While some teachers are clearly better than others, there is no requirement to be so, thus no motivation and relatively little distinction.

In fact, the teacher who genuinely places the interests of the students first and who too obviously puts forth extra effort, or who supports a student in a controversy with a staff member, may come to some grief. There have been instances in which teachers were criticized for staying after school beyond the hours stipulated in the contract with the district, the argument being that this places other teachers in a bad light.

True, personnel are assigned to evaluate teachers. Even at its best, however, this is an ineffective procedure. This writer was once evaluated by a principal who gave a rating of excellent but then commented, "I don't know what you were doing but it looked good." While formerly a teacher himself, his academic specialty was far afield from mine, and he was not familiar with the material being presented. Still, he made a conscientious effort to do what was right. Every teacher knows many evaluators who do not. Also, evaluators may only make one or two observations a year, and that may not provide a representative picture of a teacher's performance.

As Smith observed, teacher evaluation

is liable to be exercised both ignorantly and capriciously. In its nature it is arbitrary and discretionary, and the persons who exercise it, neither attending upon the lectures of the teacher themselves, nor perhaps understanding the sciences which it is his business to teach, are seldom capable of exercising it with judgement.

Furthermore, what he termed "the insolence of office" often causes the evaluators to be indifferent or arrogant in exercising their power.

In turn

the person subject to such jurisdiction is necessarily degraded by it, and, instead of being one of the most respectable, is rendered one of the meanest and most contemptible persons in the society.

While the terminology is a bit extreme, it helps explain the lack of respect that public school teachers have always had, all rhetoric to the contrary, and that to some extent they always will have while they are public hired hands.

The best teaching, according to Smith, is to be found in those areas where there are no public institutions. As an example he cites the education of women in his own day. Since there were no public schools for women in the England of two centuries ago, there was nothing "useless, absurd, or fantastical" in their education, and they were provided with that which was necessary or useful for them to learn, unlike much of the education for men.

He also concluded that change was more easily accomplished in the universities of lesser repute because teachers there relied upon their reputation for most of their income, thus they had to pay attention to public opinion.

In 1779 Thomas Jefferson, as Governor of Virginia, introduced a school bill, the first plan for a statewide school system in the New World. Calling for twenty secondary schools, Jefferson recommended that the tuition be paid by the students and, like Smith, recognizing that some parents could not afford this, proposed scholarships for needy but able students (*PSBA Bulletin*).

In *The Rights of Man*, published in London in 1792, Tom Paine carried the idea further. Believing that educational choice would promote competition among schools and lead to the success and profitability of the better ones, he proposed that the state provide an education allowance for each pupil for six years of schooling to be spent at whatever school was found most desirable.

Paine called for the expenditure of

> four pounds a year for every child under fourteen years of age; enjoining the parents of such children to send them to school, to learn reading, writing and common arithmetic; the ministers of every parish, of every denomination, to certify jointly to an office, for this purpose, that the duty is performed. (Paine 1792, I: 245)

This statement is interesting beyond its voucher aspects, for when the suggestion that ministers certify the education of children is proposed by a radical of the Revolutionary period, a different light is cast on the Establishment Clause of the Constitution's First Amendment and on the separation of church and state. It is but one indication that the interpretation of the proper relationship between the church and state, by even a harsh critic of undue influence by clerics, did not preclude cooperation between the two. It also is interesting because of President Theodore Roosevelt's later reference to Paine as "a dirty little atheist." Roosevelt should have known better. Paine also clearly stated his belief in one God and no more.

About eighty years later a French parliamentary commission examining educational finance advocated parental free choice in school selection through the use of educational allowances called the "bon scolaire." Lack of support in the French legislature caused the commission's recommendation to be shelved in 1873 (O'Donnell 1985, 101).

In 1859 the Englishman John Stuart Mill, in his essay *On Liberty*, had distinguished the difference between a state requirement for an educated citizenry and a state provision of that education. He approved of the former but not the latter, arguing that:

> A general State education is a mere contrivance for moulding people to be exactly like one another; and as the mould in which it casts them is that which pleases the predominant power of the government, whether this be a monarch, a priesthood, an aristocrat, or the majority of the existing generation; in proportion as it is efficient and successful, it establishes a despotism over the mind, leading by natural tendency to one over the body. [Mill 1966 (1859), 130]

This is exactly what government schools do, and why there is a continual struggle for power in these schools: a struggle between those who worry about "social cohesion" and "good citizenship," and those who want the freedom to have their children educated in a manner that is consistent with the values upheld in the family.

Like others, Mill called for state aid to those unable to defray the expenses of an education but at the same time wanted the schools to be kept free of government control.

He also noted that those who could provide education under government direction would be equally willing to provide it on a voluntary basis if they could be assured of support through a law making education compulsory, and if state financial aid were furnished through individuals rather than institutions. It should perhaps be recalled that, at his father's insistence and direction, Mill was himself educated outside a formal school structure.

Mill (and Stephen Arons a century and a quarter later) held that, while it could insist that a person be educated, "All attempts by the State to bias the conclusions of its citizens on disputed subjects, are evil." He stressed education as the important factor, not how that education was acquired. His proposal wouldn't automatically require schools at all.

He suggested there be annual compulsory public examinations for all children, beginning when they are young and becoming progressively more strenuous, but only to the level of an established minimum of general knowledge. Beyond that level further testing would be voluntary, with the awarding of certificates to indicate the level of proficiency obtained.

Mill's words have particular relevance for today's United States:

> Were the duty of enforcing universal education once admitted, there would be an end to the difficulties about what the State should teach, and how it should teach, which now convert the subject into a mere battlefield for sects and parties, causing the time and labour which should have been spent in educating, to be wasted in quarreling about education. If the government would make up its mind to require for every child a good education, it might save itself the trouble of providing one. It might leave to parents to obtain the education where and how they pleased, and content itself with helping to pay the school fees of the poorer classes of children, and defraying the entire school expenses of those who have no one else to pay for them. [Mill 1966 (1859), 129]

This made sense then; it makes sense now.

Notice that, with the exception of Jefferson, the thinking on this topic was primarily outside of the United States from the late eighteenth century to the late nineteenth century— Smith and Mill in England; Paine in England, America, and France; and the French legislature. This was also largely true about considerations of schooling generally. The newly formed and growing nation had little time or need for extensive concentration upon educational issues, although public and private school systems were developing.

The U.S. Supreme Court, for example, only had 3 cases involving education before 1890, and the most significant one, the *Dartmouth College* case of 1819, concerned matters of higher education. This contrasts with 140 cases between 1966 and 1984, an explosion of educational litigation that continues to accelerate.

Even *Plessy v. Ferguson* in 1896, which held constitutional the doctrine of "separate but equal" facilities for the races, was, unlike *Brown v. Board of Education* fifty-eight years later, a case involving transportation, not education. With the turn of the century, however, there were intimations of the Court's now constant point of view on educational issues.

Interstate Consolidated Street Railway Co. v. Mass. in 1907 held:

> A street railway corporation taking a legislation charter subject to all duties and restrictions set forth in all general laws relating to corporations of that class cannot complain of the unconstitutionality of a prior enacted statute compelling them to transport children attending public schools at half price.

The next year, *Quick Bear v. Leupp* allowed federal funds being administered for Indians to be applied to salaries and maintenance costs of a parochial school for Indian children. Writing for the Court, Chief Justice Melville Weston Fuller said:

> A declaration by Congress that the Government shall not make appropriations for sectarian schools does

not apply to Indian treaty and trust funds on the ground that such a declaration should be extended thereto under the religion clauses of the Federal Constitution.

Fuller added, "we cannot concede the proposition that Indians cannot be allowed to use their own money to educate their children in the schools of their own choice because the Government is necessarily undenominational."

This protection was later extended to all citizens by *Pierce*, which in 1925 held that the state may not compel public school attendance. The law was the result of an initiative adopted by the people on Nov. 7, 1922, to become effective in 1926. The plaintiffs were two Oregon corporations, The Society of Sisters and Hill Military Academy, which owned and operated schools.

William Guthrie, attorney for the appellee, recalled some educational history largely forgotten today:

Private and religious schools have existed in this country from the earliest times . . . For generations all Americans—including those who fought for liberty and independence in the eighteenth century, and who drafted the Declaration of Independence, the Northwest Ordinance of 1787, and the Constitution of the United States—were educated in private or religious schools, and mostly the latter. (514)

He also sought to correct another faulty impression:

The public school is not a "melting pot." Schools are, and obviously must be, located in given districts. If the neighborhood be American, the school there will have a similar character. If, however, it be situated in a poor and foreign quarter, the school will be attended almost entirely by children of the poor class of foreigners. The child of a foreigner is quite as likely to be assimilated and Americanized in a private or parochial school as in a public school. (517)

The case involved:

the rights of the parents and guardians who desire to send their children to such (private and religious) schools, and the rights of the children themselves . . . those rights . . . are of the very essence of personal liberty and freedom. In this day and under our civilization, the child of man is his parent's child and not the State's . . . It is not seriously debatable that the parental right to guide one's child intellectually and religiously is a most substantial part of the liberty and freedom of the parent. (518)

Associate Justice James Clark McReynolds, for the Court, accepted this reasoning:

The fundamental theory of liberty upon which all governments in this Union repose excludes any general power of the State to standardize its children by forcing them to accept instruction from public teachers only. The child is not the mere creature of the State; those who nurture him and direct his destiny have the right, coupled with the high duty, to recognize and prepare him for additional obligations. (535)

"The child is not the mere creature of the State." These words remain abstractions for Americans who have no practical option to exercise them.

School officials complaining of mandates placed upon them by higher levels of government without being given the resources to carry them out see no inconsistency in denying the same right to individual citizens. The state requires that children be educated, compels parents to accept and act upon that mandate, but does not provide funding that would permit them to do so on their own.

In 1926 England's Archbishop of Westminster, Francis Cardinal Bourne, proposed that poor parents

receive an annual . . . coupon for the cost-per-child amount, entitling the child to a place in any recognized school. . . . the adoption of this novel project would. . . relieve poor parents of a social disability

and would vivify Education by a spirit of wholesome
rivalry. (Sizer and Whitten, August 1968, 62)

During the 1920s the then Territory of Hawaii, moving in
the opposite direction, tried to force private schools to indoctrinate students. However, in *Farrington v. Tokushige,* decided Feb.
21, 1927, the U.S. Supreme Court invalidated Hawaii's law setting teacher qualifications and textbook content and requiring
teachers to pledge to "direct the mind and studies of pupils in
such schools as will tend to make them good and loyal American citizens." Aside from the constitutional question, such a
law arrogantly assumes nonpublic schools will not produce
"good and loyal American citizens" unless compelled to do so
by the government.

Associate Justice James Clark McReynolds, writing for the
Court, found this unacceptable.

> (T)he school Act and the measures adopted thereun-
> der go far beyond mere regulation of privately-sup-
> ported schools where children obtain instruction
> deemed valuable by their parents and which is not
> obviously in conflict with any public interest. They
> give affirmative direction concerning the intimate and
> essential details of such schools, entrust their control
> to public officers, and deny both owners and patrons
> reasonable choice and discretion in respect to teach-
> ers, curriculum and textbooks. Enforcement of the Act
> probably would destroy most, if not all, of them; and,
> certainly, it would deprive parents of fair opportunity
> to procure for their children instruction which they
> think important and we cannot say is harmful.
> (*Farrington*, 298)

A few years later, in 1930, in *Cochran v. La. State Board of
Education,* the Court upheld a Louisiana law providing free
textbooks for students in public and private schools. The decision held that the school children and the state were the
beneficiaries of the appropriations, not the schools. The

fundamentally important feature in this law, too often forgotten by advocates and legislators seeking to aid only the nonpublic schools, is that the free textbooks went to students in public and private schools alike.

Chief Justice Charles Evans Hughes, for the Court:

> One may scan the acts in vain to ascertain where any money is appropriated for the purchase of school books for the use of any church, private, sectarian or even public school. The appropriations were made for the specific purpose of purchasing school books for the use of the school children of the state, free of cost to them. It was for this benefit and the resulting benefit to the state that the appropriations were made. True, these children attend some school, public or private, the latter, sectarian or non-sectarian. . . . The schools, however, are not the beneficiaries of these appropriations. They obtain nothing from them, nor are they relieved of a single obligation, because of them. The school children and the state alone are the beneficiaries. (*Cochran*, 374)

It is unfortunate, and detrimental to the nation at large, that many professed advocates of education are in actuality the advocates of schools. There are supporters of the public schools and supporters of nonpublic schools. What is too often lacking are supporters of education, concerned with students rather than institutions. When a proposal benefits all students, the Courts have upheld its constitutionality. This should be true for vouchers.

In 1943 the Supreme Court handed down one of its most controversial education decisions ever, one limiting compulsion, or indoctrination, in even the public schools.

This was *West Virginia Board of Education v. Barnette*. Stressing the importance of being free from state-sponsored value inculcation, the Court said requiring students to salute the flag or repeat the pledge of allegiance violated the First and Fourteenth Amendments.

There are citizens who believe this marked a turning point in the decline of the public schools and the weakening of the patriotic and moral fiber of the nation. Yet it is debatable whether students leave school less patriotic today than formerly. This reaction also gives the schools credit for being much better in the past—the "good old days" syndrome—than they were.

Anyone recalling those days, or the reading of Bible verses in such states as Pennsylvania (also subsequently ruled unconstitutional by the Court) would realize the ritualistic nature of such exercises. They were not performed with fervor or sense of commitment but as ceremonial requirements regarded with minimal attention or interest, if not outright boredom.

Associate Justice Robert H. Jackson's opinion said:

> The Fourteenth Amendment, as now applied to the States, protects the citizen against the State itself and all of its creatures—Boards of Education not excepted ... That they are educating the young for citizenship is reason for scrupulous protection of Constitutional freedoms of the individual, if we are not to strangle the free mind at its source and teach youth to discount important principles of our government as mere platitudes. (*W. Va.*, 637)

> . . . . The very purpose of a Bill of Rights was to withdraw certain subjects from the vicissitudes of political controversy, to place them beyond the reach of majorities and officials and to establish them as legal principles to be applied by the courts. One's right to life, liberty, and property, to free speech, a free press, freedom of worship and assembly, and other fundamental rights may not be submitted to vote; they depend on the outcome of no elections. (638)

> . . . Struggles to coerce uniformity of sentiment in support of some end thought essential to their time and country have been waged by many good as well as by evil men. (640)

. . . As governmental pressure toward unity becomes greater, so strife becomes more bitter as to whose unity it shall be. Probably no deeper division of our people could proceed from any provocation than from finding it necessary to choose what doctrine and whose program public educational officials shall compel youth to unite in embracing. Ultimate futility of such attempts to compel coherence is the lesson of every such effort . . . Those who begin coercive elimination of dissent soon find themselves exterminating dissenters. Compulsory unification of opinion achieves only the unanimity of the graveyard. (641)

. . . It seems trite but necessary to say that the First Amendment to our Constitution was designed to avoid these ends by avoiding these beginnings. There is no mysticism in the American concept of the State or of the nature or origin of its authority. We set up government by consent of the governed, and the Bill of Rights denies those in power any legal opportunity to coerce that consent. Authority here is to be controlled by public opinion, not public opinion by authority. (641)

. . . (W)e apply the limitation of the Constitution with no fear that freedom to be intellectually and spiritually diverse or even contrary will disintegrate the social organization . . . We can have intellectual individualism and the rich cultural diversities that we owe to exceptional minds only at the price of occasional eccentricity and abnormal attitudes . . . freedom to differ is not limited to things that do not matter much. That would be a mere shadow of freedom. The test of its substance is the right to differ as to things that touch the heart of the existing order. (641-42)

. . . If there is any fixed star in our constitutional constellation, it is that no official, high or petty, can prescribe what shall be orthodox in politics,

> nationalism, religion, or other matters of opinion or
> force citizens to confess by word or act their faith
> therein. If there are any circumstances which present
> an exception, they do not now occur to us. (642)

This decision is quoted at length because Justice Jackson's
reasoning, accepted by the Court to this day, not only stresses
the importance of individual freedoms—for example, freedom
of speech is meaningless if one is compelled to repeat statements involuntarily, or to listen to those read by others—but it
also unintentionally raises problems of compulsory schooling.
Reconsider Jackson's words:

> Probably no deeper division of our people could pro-
> ceed from any provocation than from finding it neces-
> sary to choose what doctrine and whose program
> public educational officials shall compel youth to unite
> in embracing. Ultimate futility of such attempts to
> compel coherence is the lesson of every such effort.

Yet this is exactly what public school boards cannot avoid
despite the best of intentions. Public schools find it impossible
to avoid choosing "what doctrine and whose program" youth
must embrace. A public school cannot pledge allegiance to the
flag and not pledge allegiance, read the Bible and not read the
Bible, have *The Wizard of Oz* in the library and not have it there,
etc. Decisions must be made. Curriculums and textbooks must
be accepted. Values are projected, consciously or not. Through
the political process these programs and values are determined
by majority rule, in the ideal situation, or by the force of the
most powerful political elements in the community in the more
usual case. In either event large numbers of students and
parents, sometimes even the majority, must "unite in embracing" decisions they would reject if they had a free choice.

So why not adopt freedom of educational choice as a
national goal? It is neither impossible nor impractical. It exists
in postsecondary education where tuition vouchers in the form
of the GI Bill, Pell grants, state and other grants and
scholarships permit a large degree of personal choice.

There is, as vouchers promise for basic education, a much more diverse arrangement in postsecondary education, with technical and trade schools; two-year and four-year institutions; undergraduate, graduate, and combination colleges and universities; and corporate educational programs (the so-called "shadow higher educational system," which may be more extensive than the more formal and recognized system), and other institutions and programs.

The philosophical arguments are strong, if we believe the rhetoric about a democratic, pluralistic society. There will be mistakes; there may be schools that seem strange. But this is a price that must be paid if genius, creativity and progress are to prosper. Again recall Justice Jackson's words:

> We can have intellectual individualism and the rich cultural diversities that we owe to exceptional minds only at the price of occasional eccentricity and abnormal attitudes . . . freedom to differ is not limited to things that do not matter much. That would be a mere shadow of freedom. The test of its substance is the right to differ as to things that touch the heart of the existing order.

Four years later, the Supreme Court, in *Everson v. Board of Education*, Ewing Township, N.J., upheld New Jersey's provision reimbursing parents for money spent on public transportation for students in religious schools. The reasoning of Associate Justice Hugo Black, for the Court, was similar to that in the Louisiana case seventeen years earlier; individuals benefit, not institutions.

The decision is one more in the trend-making distinctions between students and schools, between the former as the recipients of education and the latter as the means, and not necessarily the only one, toward that end.

The Court held:

> It is much too late to argue that legislation intended to facilitate the opportunity of children to get a secular education serves no public purpose . . . The same

thing is no less true of legislation to reimburse needy parents, or all parents, for payment of the fares of their children so that they can ride in public busses to and from schools. Nor does it follow that a law has a private rather than a public purpose because it provides that tax-raised funds will be paid to reimburse individuals on account of money spent by them in a way which furthers a public program. Subsidies and loans to individuals such as farmers and home-owners, and to privately owned transportation systems, as well as many other kinds of businesses, have been commonplace practices in our state and national history.

As John Gardner once said, in another educational context, the bits and pieces of the revolution are lying all around us, waiting to be assembled.

While all the legal bits and pieces of educational freedom of choice may not yet exist, a great many do, and they await assembly, as was done over a long period of years by civil rights advocates before it was possible to win *Brown v. Board of Education* in 1954, which overturned the "separate but equal" doctrine for public facilities.

4

1955-1969
"The Role of Government in Education"

The contemporary debate over vouchers, at least in the United States, began in 1955 with a chapter by Milton Friedman, "The Role of Government in Education," which appeared in *Economics and the Public Interest,* a book edited by Robert A. Solo and published by the Rutgers University Press. Friedman is the source of two of the more controversial ideas regarding education, of which tuition vouchers is one proposal.

The other proposal calls for student aid in higher education in the form of long-term loans to be paid back as a percentage of income rather than at a fixed percentage rate. Yale and Duke Universities experimented with this in the 1970s. It was also proposed by former Pennsylvania Governor Milton Shapp, as a National Education Trust Fund (NETF), introduced in 1972 at the annual meeting of the Education Commission of the States in Los Angeles. In 1987, the Reagan administration recommended it to Congress as Income Contingency Loans (ICLs). This is another example of the proposition that significant ideas for change in a profession rarely come from those within the profession.

Debate over vouchers since 1955 has arisen not only from those in direct opposition but from those with different visions of the truth. Friedman proposed a simple voucher, with an equal amount available for each student.

A second suggestion allows for economically poor students to receive as much as three times the national average for per-pupil funding, and for more than fifty percent of all public-school students to be eligible for aid to insure majority support. If that were done it would at least double the total current instructional cost for public education, an unlikely scenario.

A source of opposition to educational choice supported by public funds is that it will permit the establishment of segregated schools. This ignores a 1958 Supreme Court decision, *Cooper v. Aaron*, in which Chief Justice Earl Warren, writing for the Court, said, "State support of segregated schools through any arrangement, management, funds or property cannot be squared with the command of the Fourteenth Amendment that no State shall deny to any person within its jurisdiction the equal protection of the laws." This has been strengthened by more than one subsequent government action, including the 1964 Civil Rights Act. Should it be further necessary to reassure anyone, it would be easy to include such a provision in a voucher authorization plan.

A more disturbing objection, in a society claiming to be democratic, is that a voucher plan would permit fast-buck operators with high-pressure tactics to take advantage of parents and students. The implied assumption is that elected or appointed government officials would not be so easily duped, and for that reason they would make better choices for citizens than those citizens would make for themselves. In other words, average citizens are incompetent to make valid decisions affecting their lives and the lives of their children. Admittedly there are philosophies based upon this assumption, but they can hardly be described as democratic. Of course, defenders of this view rarely state it quite so baldly. Instead, they speak more euphemistically about the "public welfare," "social cohesion," "the melting pot," "good citizenship," and the like.

This view is not only anti-democratic and elitist, it flies in the face of centuries of American experience and the fact that parents daily make decisions regarding feeding, clothing, and housing their children, the religious and moral values to which they will be exposed (to the degree that parents can control such factors), and decisions regarding their health and safety, which literally may be matters of life and death.

Certainly a parent who can decide whether or not a child will have an operation, or other medical procedure, should be able to decide which books the child may read, or what educational methods he or she prefers.

If the objection is that some parents will make mistakes, then it is undoubtedly correct. (Neither people nor systems are perfect, nor will they ever be.) But the suggestion implies that mistakes are not occurring now. Anyone familiar with public schools knows better. A national dropout rate approaching thirty percent, and the granting of high school diplomas to 700,000 functional illiterates annually are sufficient evidence of mistakes in the present system.

Whether a tuition voucher system or family choice would involve some mistakes is not the real question. The essential point is whether individual incompetence is greater than governmental incompetence. Mistakes by parents are individual mistakes, affecting only their children. Mistakes made by school officials may involve entire schools, districts, states, or the nation. Those by any government agency may be massive indeed.

Individual mistakes are also more easily corrected, not only because they are smaller in scale but because they are private mistakes. Governmental mistakes, being public, are rarely admitted or corrected. Should this actually occur in some instances, the length of time required to alter the system is so long that the correction would come too late for vast numbers of students.

It is also true that even the most caring and effective teachers will have a given student in class for only a limited period of time, and they will not in the future be personally aware of, or affected by, the outcome of the educational process for that student. Parents are. They know their child best; they have a lifelong continuity with them; they are affected by the ultimate result; and they, more than anyone else, are likely to make adjustments along the way, if adjustments are necessary. Public officials, and not just school officials, having made public decisions, are much more reluctant to make a change because they may be subject to criticism, or even public embarrassment or disciplinary action if they are thought to have made a serious mistake.

So while family choice is subject to debate, the claim that mistakes may be made is not relevant. The present system is already making mistakes, some of which are horrendous and clearly damaging to millions of youngsters.

Or, as a Pennsylvania state senator once said, when told that a proposal of his was no panacea; "I know it, but it is not competing with any panacea."

Family options in Denmark, a process that has an extended history, has not destroyed the public school system there, and has made possible more harmonious relations than exist in this country. It has been said that this is possible because Denmark is a small country with a more homogeneous population than the United States and that what works there will not work in a nation of 240 million people of diverse cultures. Viewed as a total system, this is true. But, unlike Denmark, we don't have a national system of education. We have 15,000 plus school districts, most with a much smaller population than Denmark, many with an equally homogeneous population, and not a few with little more discord than Denmark.

Nor is Denmark the only example that might be considered. Virtually all western democracies permit much more freedom of choice in their schooling arrangements than does the United States.

Milton Friedman noted that subsidizing institutions unavoidably means subsidizing various activities they may undertake, whether or not the government providing the funding had that in mind. State governments can hardly oversee every decision and action taken by a local school district. He also noted that mandating and providing a service can be separated, and recommended that this be done in education. The means, of course, would be the adoption of vouchers which parents could redeem with approved providers, as with the GI Bill. The providers would be responsible for students achieving the minimum level of education established by the government.

Whether this service was provided by a public or private

agency, or on a profit or nonprofit basis, should not be of concern to the government, as it was not for the millions of GIs who furthered their education with the equivalent of a voucher system. The government would only be interested in any school's meeting minimum standards.

Besides noting the GI Bill precedent in the United States, Friedman also noted that in England local authorities pay the fees for some students attending nonstate schools (which, in England, are called "public schools") and that in France, the national government does the same.

Friedman's response to the claim that such a proposal would run into administrative difficulties because of the complexity of overseeing the program is that, to the contrary, it would be even easier to administer than the present arrangement with thousands of school districts and tens of thousands of schools operating as a direct government function. This would be particularly so if vouchers were a federal program, as he recommended, and as most advocates prefer.

The key is to consider what the government should finance in contrast to what it should administer. In the past thirty years that question has been reviewed in greater detail, and governments at various levels are increasingly making funds or credits directly available to people to make their own choices rather than having the decision made for them. Medicaid, Medicare, Food Stamps, and rental rebates are among practices that have become common since the mid-1950s.

Friedman did not, however, advocate the elimination of all educational institutions operated by government. The higher education analogy again applies.

Governments directly support and operate colleges and universities at the same time they provide grants (vouchers) to students which may be used at a wide variety of institutions. The object is not to abandon one rigid approach only to supplant it with another, but to carefully consider those circumstances in which one approach or another is most desirable.

Virgil Blum, writing in 1958 in support of the voucher concept, cited for examples not only the GI Bill (technically, the Servicemen's Readjustment Act of 1944) but also its 1952 successor for Korean War veterans, the War Orphans' Educational

Assistance Act of 1956, and, perhaps most significantly, the Legislative Reorganization Act of 1946, which provided for the education of Congressional pages. Constituents should have the same privileges as Congressional pages.

Blum added that veterans had used their educational benefits not only at 481 nonsectarian institutions of higher learning but at 474 Protestant, 265 Catholic, and 5 Jewish schools. At the time he was writing, 36,000 veterans had used this funding source to become members of the clergy, mostly Protestant.

No question was raised about constitutionality, the separation of church and state, or whether this freedom of choice was anything but a benefit to the individuals involved. How they elected to exercise this choice was their business alone, as long as they actually attended a recognized institution and received the education for which the government was paying.

A Tuition Voucher Act would permit those setting out on life's journey to exercise freedom of choice just as the Social Security Act permits those in the later stages of life to do instead of being relegated to state institutions or the local "poor house," as was for so long the custom.

Blum said no other Western democracy "has so adamantly stood face-to-face with its principles of liberty and refused to recognize in them the simple conclusions of educational freedom" (Blum 1958, 130).

A move to establish this principle in the U.S. came in 1963, when Rep. James J. Delaney of New York reintroduced a measure to appropriate twenty dollars annually for two years to pay part of the costs of educating each elementary and secondary pupil in the nation. While twenty dollars is a minimal figure at best, it needs to be remembered that costs per pupil were then measured in hundreds of dollars annually, not thousands of dollars.

Robert Hutchins said the idea "should satisfy everybody, except those who hold that a church-related school is the same thing as a church" (Dahl 1964, 323).

A market system should result in smaller educational units than presently exist. It isn't likely that an entrepreneur would create an educational district with ten thousand pupils, much less a system the size of the New York City school district. Nor is there any evidence that schools containing thousands of pupils would result, and such schools are common in the public system. Even the present private schools for the rich, in which money is of relatively little concern, have smaller buildings and student bodies.

Smaller units mean more units, more flexibility, more innovation, the absence of centralized administrative control (with no considerations for well-meaning paternalism or beneficence) and much greater variety. Ironically, this possibility of greater variety is one of the fears that voucher opponents raise. They say that, even if racial and other forms of discrimination are avoided, the creation of great numbers of small schools responsive to student and parent choices will increase the likelihood of ideological or other forms of separation. But isn't this supposed to be a main feature of a pluralistic society? How can pluralism and conformity be consistently defended at the same time?

There are Americans who lack a basic commitment to democracy and pluralism. They oppose, and are afraid of, those who think or act differently from themselves, those they accuse of having "foreign ideas." Often these so-called "foreign ideas" have originated in this country, but those who are fearful don't understand or accept them.

It is difficult to help such people overcome their fear because they are unaware of the narrowness out of which it comes and deny it if challenged. They consider themselves good Americans without defining the term. Their concept of "good" is someone essentially like themselves. And it isn't just members of the Ku Klux Klan or other fringe groups who are guilty of this social blindness.

Today, what many regard as an inherent danger in the voucher system would, in a truly democratic and pluralistic society, be looked upon as one of its major advantages.

> At a time when concern is expressed over increasing pressures toward social conformity perhaps an

educational system should seek that form of organization suited to maximum cultural variation. (Tope 1965, 181)

The same may be true of another common objection made in connection with vouchers: that parents are too apathetic to actively participate in a market system of choice. The critics who raise this objection ignore the conditions in the present system that suggest there may be much to be apathetic about. Also, they don't seem to recognize in their objection any evidence of their own anti-democratic elitism.

Actually, few elements or individuals within the system truly desire the active participation of students and parents unless it serves the status quo. One of the evidences of this is the gradual weakening of parent-teacher associations in those districts where parents have tried to assert themselves even modestly, or where votes on policy decisions have not ratified the position of the local teachers' organization. If parents' views were welcomed, if what they desire for their children were acceptable to local school authorities, the number of court cases over ideological and methodological issues would not be growing at an exponential rate.

When so modest a proposal as open enrollment among district schools on a space-available basis is a cause for concern among teachers and other school officials, parent "apathy" becomes not only a more understandable phenomenon but a predictable and reasonable one.

School officials, for example, often bemoan the lack of attendance at such a harmless affair as parent night, when parents are encouraged to come to school, meet with the teachers of their children, and ask questions or express their views on district or teacher policies and actions.

Two factors are generally ignored in this wringing of hands.

First, if all parents really came to these sessions and said what they thought, and challenged the system, the moaning would escalate sharply and parent night might even become a thing of the past.

Second, even if parents did not create problems at such

sessions, the idea that all the parents of the thirty or so students an elementary teacher may have—not to mention the 150 or more assigned to a secondary teacher—can possibly meet with the teacher and have a meaningful discussion in the usual two-hour period devoted to such sessions is unrealistic.

Like so many aspects of the public schools, parent night is primarily a public relations device, a means by which parents can allegedly have the opportunity to be heard. If they fail to do so they are called apathetic.

How different it would be if a group of parents, rather than showing up at parents night to argue with a teacher, or petitioning a school board to address real or imagined grievances, could say, "We're taking our children, and the money that accompanies them, out of this school and out of this district, and transferring them to a school more agreeable to our wishes."

Either the school or school district would satisfactorily respond in some way to student and parental concerns or they would not. In the first case, students and parents would achieve some satisfaction. In the second, the students would be transferred to a school that would be more responsive to their wishes. Either way, the student benefits. Those who really believe that students are the ultimate reason for the existence of schools cannot argue with that. The clincher is that such responsive schools would be both more effective academically and more efficient financially.

Anyone who expects a state-owned and operated educational institution to be responsive, more effective or more efficient has simply not stopped to contemplate the vast morass of laws, rules, regulations, policies, and restrictions placed upon the public system—the list of which grows significantly longer each year.

In government schools everyone who has an idea of what might be an educational good must seek it not only for his or her own children but for everyone else's as well.

Even universal agreement about state schooling does not guarantee that appropriate action will be taken to improve conditions. For example, everyone probably agrees that good teachers should be retained and that poor teachers should either be upgraded or released. To make this possible it would seem reasonable to expect teachers to be evaluated. However, universal agreement does not make mandates successful.

The first problem in confronting this issue is that in a public system such evaluations would have to be somewhat public; therefore, both the evaluator and the evaluated would most likely seek to avoid anything that might be publicly embarrassing.

The second, and even more basic, difficulty is that passing a law mandating teacher evaluation by local districts does not assure that it will be implemented in a way that a genuine evaluation will take place. Local districts and officials obviously go through the necessary steps to satisfy the law; that is, teachers are evaluated as often as the law requires—proper forms are filled out and teachers are rated as satisfactory or unsatisfactory, the usual common options. However, since it is almost unheard of for anyone to complain about a satisfactory rating, and it is almost equally unheard of for anyone to accept an unsatisfactory rating without causing problems, with very few exceptions teachers are rated as satisfactory.

In short, unless local school officials want to truly evaluate their teachers to insure a good educational experience for all students, no legal mandate will have the slightest effect upon them beyond requiring the necessary pretenses and formalities.

Again, how different it would be if students who believe they have an unsatisfactory, if not incompetent, teacher could simply withdraw from that teacher and go to one that is acceptable. No evaluations. No charades. No public embarrassment. No grievance procedures, hearings, legal expenses, or— that euphemism for preventing change—"due process." Competent teachers would have students and income. Incompetent teachers would have to make adjustments or change careers.

Because unsatisfactory and unnecessary staff of all kinds would not be utilized in a soundly based educational environment, *some in the educational establishment* fear the freedom of choice that comes from funding students rather than institutions.

The phrase *some in the educational establishment* needs to be emphasized because polls have consistently shown that significant percentages of teachers and administrators favor vouchers. The percentages were even higher before some professionals were scared off by the negative statements of their organizations. These organizations, through their leaders and staff, have their own interests to promote.

Even though teachers would need these organizations to represent them under a voucher system, their dependency would not be so great. Today, for example, the organizations representing teachers are much larger in size, budget, and staffing than are those representing other professional groups. The reason is simple. Today most teachers are not truly professionals. They are public employees who, instead of working directly for constituents, work for a third-party employer, frequently under a more or less lengthy and complicated contract. Furthermore, the largest single group of the organization's staff are those involved in negotiating and servicing contracts, handling grievance procedures, working on arbitration cases, ensuring "due process," and managing strikes.

If teachers were ever to become truly professionals, those legal matters and related jobs, would for the most part disappear. This is why the teachers' organizations condemn vouchers and persuade their members to do so without once thoroughly studying the question or permitting a pilot project.

Teachers who are delegates to conventions and assemblies that adopt policy positions should think more carefully about what they are doing and how they are voting. When they condemn "deleterious" programs, they should raise the questions: deleterious to whom, under what circumstances, and what is the evidence? Maybe, in fact, they are faced with a challenge. Then again, maybe they are not. A competent, caring teacher has nothing to fear from vouchers, nothing to lose, and very much to gain. Unfortunately, today tuition-voucher advocates often stress advantages to students and parents and ignore the role of teachers or view vouchers as a way to keep teachers under control. This antagonizes teachers and is philosophically wrong. It is also untrue, for teacher autonomy and professional status would more likely be strengthened. The fact that vouchers provided students and parents with the essential element of choice, would not be a threat to good teachers. Also, they would still need organizations to represent them, even as doctors, lawyers and other professional groups do.

While he didn't mean it in the context presented here, Braulio Alonso, National Education Association President, was correct when he told the 1968 national convention that "It is the time to decide whether to so shape our profession and our nation so that every teacher, every administrator, every child will have the freedom to exercise the rights and command the respect which belong to every human being. We must be committed to this action."

Braulio surely meant every word of that. But full implementation of his belief can only be achieved by altering the conditions to make it possible. The last thing the present system of schooling allows, virtually anywhere in the world, is the opportunity for anyone to "have the freedom to exercise the rights and command the respect which belong to every human being."

The greatest and most unexpected result of a voucher system probably would not be the freedom of choice for students and parents but the freedom of choice for teachers. At last their individual differences, skills, and philosophies would permit them to create the circumstances they feel would best serve the interests of the children with whom they work, and for whom most of them do have a genuine affection and concern.

The power of an idea that has survived for over two centuries, and that can attract a Christopher Jencks, a Milton Friedman, and a wide variety of other thinkers, should demonstrate the need to give it a fair trial if we are to truly determine its effects.

Another judicial step in assuring the constitutional acceptability of the voucher system came in 1968 when the Supreme Court, in *Allen v. Board of Education*, upheld a state's provision of textbooks to all students in grades seven to twelve, including those in private schools. The Court maintained the consistency of its position, noting that the law provided textbooks generally "and the financial benefit is to parents and children, not to schools."

The politics of a school system mandated, centralized,

owned, funded, and operated by the state has perhaps rarely been as succinctly stated as it was by Christopher Jencks in 1968:

> The essential issue in the politics of American education has always been whether laymen or professionals would control the schools . . . Professionals always want more money for the schools, while laymen almost always want to trim the budget . . . Professionals want a curriculum which reflects their own ideas about the world, and this often means a curriculum that embodies "liberal" ideas and values they picked up at some big university . . . Laymen frequently oppose this demand, insisting that the curriculum should reflect conservative local mores. (Jencks 1968, 132-33)

In the same article, Jencks noted that the Supreme Court permitted the government to contract with Catholic hospitals to care for charity patients in the nineteenth century. He raises the logical question as to why, if that was true then, and if the federal government can today contract with a religious university or hospital to conduct scientific research—to which no one has objected—it should not be equally permissible for government to contract with a religious institution to teach physics or reading to younger students?

Alumni of parochial schools, despite the fewer resources seem to be as successful in life, are a bit better educated, and have somewhat better jobs than their co-religionists who attended public schools. Also, Jencks cited a 1964 survey which concluded that parochial school students seem a bit more liberal than those from public schools. This is not to say that parochial schools are necessarily better than public schools. It is sufficient to know that they certainly are no worse. Thus the burden of compulsory public schooling is placed upon its defenders, not on those advocating choice.

Clearly, the exercising of the right of choice remains an abstraction only if student assistance is not further developed and expanded, and as Kenneth Clark has observed, there isn't much chance of improving public education unless alternatives to the present system are developed.

That minorities and the economically disadvantaged would favor vouchers should not be surprising.

More than twenty years ago, Rodger Hurley observed, "Although the system of public education in America is certainly not solely responsible for the failure of the poor to learn and for their over-representation in Special Education classes for the mentally retarded, it is more responsible than any other single institution in our society" (Hurley 1969, 91).

Those who feel compelled to defend the present system continue to attack any serious movement toward competition and choice among alternatives as likely to destroy the public schools. More than one critic has noted this shows a distinct lack of faith in the system they are attempting to protect. As Kenneth Clark has remarked, competition should only strengthen that which deserves to survive.

It isn't too likely that worthwhile available options will be the ones to fail. Clark also has a point in suggesting that public education should be defined as that which is in the public interest rather than merely that which is government controlled. If the present system is not better than other educational practices why should it survive, or even dominate? And if it is the better of possible approaches, will it not continue to flourish on its merits rather than because of coercion?

Is it the system we should be most concerned with, or is it students and the public interest? Was the GI Bill not in the public interest because many of its beneficiaries attended private, or nongovernment, institutions, or because thousands used it to enter the ranks of the clergy? It certainly did not destroy public higher education, which now educates not only a greater number but a far greater proportion of students than it did at the end of World War II. Nor have vouchers destroyed basic education in those areas where it has been implemented.

Is a system that is inefficient, that clearly harms many students, that expends funds but resists being held accountable, that maintains the bill-paying public is not competent to judge the quality of the product it is receiving, and that blames society for its failures while claiming credit for its successes, in the public interest? Clark and others say no.

Other nations have demonstrated that alternatives are possible.

Denmark's compulsory education began in 1814. From the beginning it was permissible for parents to have their children tutored or attend schools other than those of the state, a right finally clarified in the United States by *Pierce* in 1925. But the Danes have gone further. The government provides financial and other aid to private schools meeting certain curriculum and health standards.

It should relieve the fears of public school advocates here to know that the great majority of Danes send their children to state schools, that only about seven percent of school-age children go to private schools, and that even fewer are educated at home, a legal right in that country. The existence of this option, and its utilization by a minority, relieves pressure on the state system because those who are dissatisfied need not struggle to bring everyone around to their view, or otherwise challenge the majority status quo.

As a result Denmark does not have the school conflicts increasingly common here. Danish educational discussions are more likely to be of curriculum, funding, or teaching practices rather than discussions that deal with clashes between the school and community groups, or between teachers and administrators (Fuchs 1969, 55).

Funding of students and other alternatives does not mean the end of public education. It has not done so elsewhere, or in higher education here. In the latter instance, the public sector has grown to such an extent that those who wonder about their future are in private higher education.

5

1970
The OEO Proposal

On May 4, 1970, the U.S. Supreme Court, in *Walz v. Tax Commission,* ruled that tax deductions and exemptions for churches are constitutional, as are tax deductions for personal contributions to support religious worship, because: "Freedom from taxation for two centuries has not led to an established church or religion and on the contrary has helped to guarantee the free exercise of all forms of religious belief." If direct contributions to churches are constitutional, similar contributions to church-affiliated schools should be also. Since this is not the case, perhaps church-affiliated schools should stop charging tuition and receive funds from contributions made directly to the church. Admittedly, this does seem needlessly roundabout, especially since such schools are certainly less directly involved in any church and state issue than are the churches themselves.

In 1970 there was an upturn in the attention given to tuition vouchers, largely because in December 1969 the U.S. Office of Economic Opportunity had given a grant to the Center for the Study of Public Policy to prepare a report on "education vouchers." Consequently, in March 1970, the Center submitted a preliminary report to OEO suggesting the possible use of vouchers at the elementary school level and recommending that OEO try to establish a five- to eight-year demonstration

63

project to test this theory. The Center then undertook an eight-month feasibility study of such a project and, in December 1970, issued a 348-page document, *Education Vouchers*.

The report rejected the plan for a simple voucher providing a set amount of money for each student. Instead, it recommended a regulated compensatory voucher—a voucher with certain restrictions and providing more money for some students than others, determined on the basis of special needs.

The search for a willing school district included letters to school superintendents in all cities with a 1960 population in excess of 150,000.

Not one of the districts contacted could be persuaded to attempt a pilot project as planned. One district, Alum Rock in California, finally agreed, but only with a number of restrictions. This subsequently led some opponents to say the innovation was a failure. Even some supporters said it wasn't a *real* tuition voucher project, despite some success.

Although a number of persons were involved in the production of the final report to OEO, and it was admitted there wasn't unanimity concerning its contents, the person most often mentioned in connection with the report is Christopher Jencks, at that time the president of the Center and an Associate Professor of Education at Harvard.

The existence of the study and the search for an adventurous school district can be credited with one major accomplishment: for the first time, vouchers became a subject of significant debate. Predictably, supporters of public schooling quickly attacked the proposal, in some instances so quickly that it was obvious they had given little thought to the matter but were acting primarily from a perceived self-interest. Just as predictably, many supporters were equally quick to come to a decision, making it apparent that either they definitely opposed the present public system or they individually supported one of many nonpublic institutions and systems, and saw a possible chance to obtain the government funding and support they had long been seeking.

Many of the arguments, both pro and con, are made by people who do not convey much knowledge either of the history of the idea or of examples around the world that might be studied; neither do they seem to realize the possible impact of free choice on public schooling as a system or on those serving that system.

For example, some arguments for vouchers seem to be motivated more by anti-teacher sentiments than by careful consideration of the central issue. If there are persons acting from such sentiments, they need not go to all the bother of promoting tuition vouchers, which may or may not ultimately be successful; all they need do is to be elected to the school board in almost any district in the land. The odds are they will find kindred spirits already there who will willingly join them in an assault on teachers.

Much of the reasoning in the debate centered on points already discussed: the pros cited the GI Bill and experiences in other countries (although few carried the connection back to Adam Smith or even into the nineteenth century); the cons expressed fear that diversity in education would threaten the unity and stability of the nation and would bring an end to the public school system.

One of the characteristics of the debate, not unique to the voucher issue, was the frequency with which both supporters and opponents stated with dogmatic certainty what the results of such a plan would be, without troubling to present a shred of evidence or a carefully reasoned statement in support of either view. For example, supporters often assert that vouchers and a system of choice are sure to remove control of the schools from the professionals and return it to the parents, even though this is not now generally the case in either American private basic education or higher education.

That some people who presently have a great deal of control or authority in the present system would lose it, and others would gain, if the system were significantly changed, seems apparent. That is in the nature of significant change. But that is not the same as having professionals lose power as a group and seeing parents gain it collectively. That is doubtful, to say the least. As a matter of record, in the Alum Rock project (which is covered in detail later), the teachers gained power. Not only did teachers gain power but parents in Alum Rock were generally satisfied with the changes that occurred. This, too, should have been anticipated because they agreed to a process by which everyone gained, including the students. It is the desirable win-win model, although everyone does not gain quite the same thing. On the basis of the Alum Rock evidence, therefore, teachers should consider supporting vouchers, whatever their organizations may say.

Teachers gain power, in a professional sense, when their customers or clients, the students, have a choice. Teachers are freer to develop pedagogical approaches that they think have merit. In these matters, parents tend to be deferential to teachers, just as they would be to doctors, hesitant to tell a doctor what medicine or treatment should be prescribed for their child's illness.

As might be expected, when teachers gain power over the educational process, the parents are prepared to accept this because they themselves acquire additional options. The more variations teachers create in exercising their power, the more options the parents have in choosing an educational system for their children. This is really what most students and parents want, and it is what they should receive.

When the professionals develop the programs they believe are correct for students, they will dialogue not only with other teachers but also with their potential clientele. This means that students and parents will become informed about what is available and will be able to make a suitable choice.

What a contrast to the present system in which there are precious few choices for any teacher, student, or parent. In the case of the teachers, most of the deciding is not only done for them but it is done without any serious attempt to determine their knowledge, preferences, or interests at all. If a school district needs three new high school history teachers, three are hired, randomly assigned to classrooms, and provided with textbooks which, with luck, are less than ten years old. At the beginning of the year, they will receive the roster of the 150 or so students assigned to them. Most likely, they will not have had the students before and, unless the teacher has an unusual memory, a considerable number of weeks or months will go by before names can be associated with faces. The year may even end without teachers getting to know some of the students at all. Most of the rest they will know only superficially. And they will probably never have any of them again.

During my own years of working with teachers I have identified virtually none who like the present system. Do they like the conditions under which they serve? No. Is this the way they think it should be? No. If they had the opportunity to design their own system would it be like the present one? No.

Yet when push comes to shove and a proposal comes forth that might extensively change the system or conditions under which the teachers can function, they go along with their organizations, which invariably line up in opposition. Fears overcome hope, even though the proposal for a voucher system—were it ever to be given a fair shot—might free teachers from the system, from their organizations' control, and from their own fears.

In any event, with the appearance of the OEO proposal and the attempt to find a school district willing to participate voluntarily on some basis over a period of several years, it became apparent the federal government was serious. The possibility of the adoption of vouchers appeared real, and an avalanche of articles, speeches and even books began to appear.

Aside from the educational merits of a voucher system, its adoption would hopefully end the ongoing and intensifying controversy over state funding for religious schools. In recent years this controversy has perhaps been more divisive than at any time in our history. If the Founding Fathers could return, they would be astounded by how the Establishment Clause of the First Amendment, a provision to reduce animosities among a diverse population, has been used to exacerbate them instead.

Under a voucher system, there would no longer be a need for public funds to go directly to religious affiliated schools, whether for tuition, textbooks, transportation, or any other purpose. Funds allocated to individuals would make support to any school a private decision rather than a political one, in line with the GI Bill and other forms of student grants.

Many of the nation's founders were not religious in the conventional, organizational sense. They tended to be rationalists, agnostics, and Deists. Yet they did not hesitate to make allusions to a Supreme Being. The idea that books of American history would someday appear without reference to the religious motivations and beliefs of the Pilgrims, the Puritans, the Quakers, and of the founders themselves, all in the name of separation of church and state, would probably have been incomprehensible to them—as it is incomprehensible to many Americans today.

Possible resolution of the church-state question is sufficient reason to give vouchers and educational choice a try. Robert Cunningham says it is difficult to see how schools organized to meet parents' interests, including religious and philosophical preferences, could displease anyone except those who are determined to maintain the present coercive system.

The myth that the public-school system serves the general public which controls it with the right to vote has as much validity as the equivalent myth that stockholders are served by the corporations in which they hold stock and which they control with the voting rights the stock grants them. With the exceptions that sometimes occur under unusual circumstances, corporation executives and their self-perpetuating boards control corporations, and school administrators and school boards control school systems.

Whether the parent-citizen-voter is one of millions, as in New York City, or one of only a thousand in some small town, his or her individual impact on the schools is so minimal as to be essentially nonexistent. If the school district is really small, with only a few hundred voters, the individual is still outvoted hundreds to one. Moreover, there is probably some person of wealth or influence—like the local banker or owner of the community's major business—who still dominates from behind the scenes, whatever the democratic theory may be. Anyone who has tried to alter school policy, if only for their own child, has learned this fact the hard way.

On a personal level, would you have located the schools in your district where they are? Would you have built them as they are? Would you operate them as they do? Would you have selected your children's present teachers? Would you have chosen the textbooks they use? Would you place the same emphasis on the extracurricular activities as your child's school does? Would you send your child to a school miles from home if you had a choice? Would you pay the taxes you do to support the system you have? Are you satisfied with your local schools? If your answer is no, you are an advocate of freedom of choice.

If we consider current reports on the public's dissatisfaction with the state of education in the United States, it seems safe to assume that any learning environment that was controlled by parents and teachers would not be a replica of the current school system.

The next time someone tells you that parents do not have sufficient interest in their children to assume greater responsibility for their education, ask that person if they themselves would have sufficient interest to do so. If they say yes, as they probably will, ask them how they reached the conclusion that the majority of other parents care less for their children than they do.

If this person is an educator decrying the apathy of other citizens, you might also inquire as to why it is (as a matter of record) that public school teachers across the nation send their own children to nonpublic schools at a higher rate than does the general public. If those who know public schooling best, and who earn their living from it, do not favor it for their own children, by what reasoning do they insist that it be mandatory for others?

How can they send their children to those nonpublic schools that are said to be "havens for rich folks' kids," "divisive," "centers of bigotry," "undemocratic," and guilty of all the other labels that are applied to them, charges that have not been documented and that studies indicate are not generally true?

Wherever there is free choice, differences of opinion will occur and differences of opinion are divisive. Hitler and Stalin knew that the pluralism of democracy is inherently divisive. However, they did not realize how unified we can become to defend our *right* to differ. *E pluribus unum.*

Robert L. Cunningham made the point that if the public school is not "divisive," it can only not be so at the expense of freedom, and is that a price we want to pay? There are those who say yes. To those we should pose the questions If conformity and standardization are the policy, where are the new ideas to come from? If the majority is to rule, should not the minority be left free to seek to inform that majority and persuade it toward an opinion it does not presently hold but perhaps should?

> (T)he conception that government should be guided by majority opinion makes sense only if that opinion is independent of government . . . There is no evidence that a school system where parents have a choice between alternative types of schooling, will fail to mirror our society as it is, or make rational discussion more difficult. (Cunningham 1970, 17)

Cunningham answers the question as to why those who established this country did not establish government support for a private-school system: there were no large-scale educational systems, public or private, until well into nineteenth century so it was not a question that came up in the eighteenth.

Well, one might ask, why was a public system developed when schooling did emerge? For one thing, in a largely agricultural society problems of transportation and communication prohibited a more innovative approach. For another, massive immigration in the nineteenth century raised fears that public schools seemed to help resolve. Then, says Cunningham, many Catholics who fought for private schools did so on the grounds of Roman Catholic rights rather than on the grounds of general parental rights. This is a mistake many, and not just Catholics, still make. Freedom of educational choice may be debatable but if it is a good idea, it is good for everyone.

A different mistake was made by nineteenth-century Protestants. Belonging to the dominant religious group of the time, they believed that public schools could be Christian though non-sectarian, a belief many of their heirs have come to regret. Finally, intellectuals were impressed with the Prussian public-school system without giving thought to why that system developed as it had.

Cunningham was equally concerned with today's liberal intellectuals who, as he saw it, express concern with individual liberties at the same time that they favor government action inhibiting individual initiative. He did say that "if this group ever came down on the side of effective parental choice, the battle would be over," but he was not overly confident this would happen.

An example of liberal philosophy in action was the vehement support of the American Civil Liberties Union for the right of American Nazis to parade in a Jewish community in Illinois, along with an equally vehement opposition to the right of American parents to control the educational destiny of their children. Of course, in a free society the ACLU has a right to be so stubbornly inconsistent, but one marvels at its powers of rationalization.

Cunningham saw a corresponding dichotomy in the position of conservatives, who tend to oppose innovation yet want to reduce the influence of government.

Major religious groups have their own inconsistencies. They often favor choice for themselves yet are unwilling to grant it to others. Unfortunately there is sometimes a human tendency to forego a benefit rather than extend it to others with whom we disagree. We would rather do without than share.

The forces that would benefit from vouchers are potentially formidable. If united they could probably overcome the inertia and resistance of the present system. *If.* "Aye, there's the rub."

Defenders of the present system are well organized, constantly operative, and ever alert. Supporters of educational choice are relatively unorganized, fragmented, sporadic in their efforts, and frequently disagree with each other. Not surprisingly, the OEO found it impossible to make a true test of the voucher concept, although it came close. Cunningham hoped that educational economy, achievable by creating vouchers worth less than per-pupil costs of public schools, would be a powerful motivator. So far that hope has been in vain. Today's costs are considerably higher than in 1970, even in constant dollars, but the system persists.

James Coleman added his support, saying:

> There is, really, only one method of financing education which can bring about approximate equality of

educational resources . . . This is a return of resources to each family, in the form of tuition vouchers. (Coons, Clune, et al., 1970, XIII-XIV)

John Holt stressed this point:

It is because our relationship with the public is not voluntary, not based on mutual consent, that we are not allowed to be professional. Because the parents. . . have . . . no other option, they are bound to try to make us say or do in those classes whatever they want, whether we like it or not. (Holt 1970, 265)

From Kenneth Boulding:

As long as the near-monopoly of the public school system exists intact, substantial technical changes are unlikely . . . A change in methods of finance to one which subsidizes the student rather than the school might indeed set off drastic changes in the organization of the whole industry. (Johns 1970, 26)

In California, State Representatives William Campbell and Leon Ralph sponsored a tuition grants bill, which received the expected opposition of public-school forces, but gained the endorsement of columnist James J. Kilpatrick. He admitted, however, that "Its hour hasn't come."

The June 20, 1970 issue of *America* magazine added its endorsement: "American education needs new energy and new creativity. Experiments are necessary, and Prof. Jencks and his associates have designed one of the best we have seen in a long time."

So did *The Nation* of June 29, with some caution. "Giving consumers the means to purchase educational services may be a valuable proposal."

In the July 4 issue of *The New Republic*, Jencks spoke out in defense of his proposal.

Today's public school has a captive clientele. . . . The state, the local board, and the school administration establish regulations to ensure that no school will do anything to offend anyone of political consequence. . . . The voucher system seeks to free schools from these managerial constraints by eliminating their monopolistic privileges.

He also noted the concern that giving parents a choice would begin an educational equivalent of Gresham's Law, in which poor schools would drive out the good ones, an argument he regarded as lacking supporting evidence. While he admitted there are existing private schools of inferior quality, he concluded that their quality is generally at least equal to that of the public schools, which also have some very poor models in their ranks.

He added that much depends on how the term "public" is defined. If it means schools that accept all students within a commuting distance, there are few truly public schools in the nation within the public system. School district lines, exclusive suburbs, and wealthy neighborhoods, even the lines of assignment for a particular school within a district, determine access to good "public" schools so that they are often as restrictive as "private" schools, if not more so. Vouchers, therefore, might extend access rather than restrict it.

As for "destroying the public schools," Jencks noted that most wealthy parents, who do not need vouchers, and would not be able to add any personal funds to them under his proposal, continue to send their children to public schools as long as they are reasonably adequate.

Of course, added to this motivation is the often exclusive nature of many so-called public schools because of characteristics already noted, such as the ability to live in a wealthy neighborhood where the better schools are found.

In the view of Frederick Treesh, "The long-range potential is awesome," although he also saw possible problems.

Newsweek, calling it "Pay-as-You-Go Schooling," concluded that

the success or failure of vouchers will depend ultimately on parental response. And for all their complaints about public education, it remains to be seen whether most parents are prepared to accept the fearsome responsibility of buying schooling for their children.

The magazine included Jencks' reply that the parents of millions of youngsters in nonpublic schools apparently have no such problem making choices.

A. Stafford Clayton provided information on experiences in other nations. The Netherlands has had general subsidies since 1920 and France since 1951. England is yet another nation that subsidizes parents' choice.

Robert J. Havighurst, terming vouchers "The Unknown Good," estimated that not more than one parent in five would use freedom of choice to bypass the nearest school. Even so, he hoped to see vouchers tried. He felt that if even fifteen percent of a cross-section of the nation's youngsters tried it, it would be an impressive program.

At its annual meeting, held in San Francisco in 1970, the Representative Assembly of the National Education Association, by voice vote and without serious review or debate, unhesitatingly adopted Resolution 70-13 which declared

that the so-called voucher plan . . . could lead to racial, economic, and social isolation of children and weaken or destroy the public school system. The Association urges the enactment of federal and state legislation prohibiting the establishment of such plans. (*Today's Education*)

Ironically, this was adopted on July 4, Independence Day.

As president of the 100,000-member Pennsylvania State Education Association and chairman of its delegation, I expressed a contrary view in the next issue of the *Pennsylvania School Journal*:

Public education in the United States is under an everincreasing attack and is being challenged as never before. To take an ostrichlike view of these challenges, as the NEA Representative Assembly did on some issues at San Francisco in July—issues such as performance contracts and tuition vouchers . . . will be to no avail. We should be willing to take part in any educational experiments and be quick to accept those that show value. (Kirkpatrick 1970, 71)

That little serious study was given to the issue was demonstrated by the argument supporting the resolution. The day before the resolution came to the floor, the leadership distributed a memo urging its condemnation. The principal reason given was that this would only give more money to those who could already afford to send their children to nonpublic schools.

Since the OEO-Jencks proposal stated that anyone accepting a voucher would be restricted to money it provided, and prohibited from adding any funds of their own, it was apparent the NEA leadership/staff did not carefully read the proposal, did not understand it, or misrepresented it.

Whatever the cause, the position was, and is, disturbing to some educators, who cannot understand this fear of seeking better ways to educate children.

The opposition by public-school forces is undoubtedly a major reason many others are so strongly for alternatives.

We have wasted too much time and energy on the state's schools, and we have failed to consider or create alternatives. Now it is time to cut loose from the myth. We must realize once and for all that, given the real inner condition of the young, the state's schools are no place to try to help them. (Peter Marin)

It is conceivable that single public school systems might, on their own initiative, introduce the kind of pluralism that the voucher system is designed to achieve . . . And yet the pressure within a single system is likely to be the other way. (Peter Schrag)

If we are to be miseducated, I prefer that it be my mistake rather than the state's. This is one reason why I am so much in favor of public independent education and the educational voucher system. (Margot Hentoff)

In October 1970, *Education U.S.A.* reported that a Gallup poll had found forty-three percent of the public supported vouchers. Presidents of the United States are elected with less than forty-three percent of the eligible vote.

Peter A. Janssen, while supporting vouchers, was a realist:

School systems are not given to making difficult changes overnight, and it may be many years before any of them embark on a voucher program on a large enough scale to reverse the despair that now grips schools in poverty areas. That despair, however, certainly is not going to be lessened by maintaining the status quo.

John W. S. Eurich, from Vanderbilt University in Tennessee, was one of those who wrote a letter to the editor of *Christian Century.* Speaking of the public-school system, he raised the question as to

whether . . . the all-pervasive monolith is working for our own good . . . It is time for the monolith to be broken and Christopher Jencks's voucher system would be an excellent way to do it . . .

Douglas M. Still, of the Department of Social Justice for the National Council of Churches of Christ, was another:

The fear that American families are too ignorant and indifferent to be entrusted with their children's educational welfare seems to me insufferably arrogant . . .

The year concluded with challenges presented, questions raised, fears aroused, and nothing resolved.

6

1971-1972
Court Decisions and Survey Results

The debate over vouchers gathered momentum in 1971. The OEO-sponsored study in 1970 and the search for school districts willing to participate in a voucher project aroused both support and opposition. The effect of the opposition soon became apparent.

A March 1970 opinion survey of school administrators, which appeared in the January 1971 issue of *Nation's Schools*, indicated that forty-three percent approved the voucher concept, and many were willing to attempt it in their district. By 1971, however, this support was reduced by more than half, to only twenty percent, largely because of warnings from their associations—whose leadership must work on behalf of the perpetuation of their groups in a way that will not diminish their power.

Rank-and-file teachers did better. Forty-five percent of the teachers still favored vouchers, despite the year-old NEA stance (*Phi Delta Kappan*, May 1971, 512). Since the NEA is a very vocal defender of teachers' rights to professional participation and autonomy, it is strange that they would oppose the desire of so many teachers to be empowered to make their own decisions and to work directly with students and parents.

That the NEA would survive such a change should be obvious. That it would, however, be affected should be equally obvious. There would be no more collective bargaining, no more processing of grievances, no more (or definitely fewer) strikes, among other things. This, in turn, would require a significant alteration of staff structure and functions. The same, of course, would be true for the American Federation of Teachers which poses as being even more militant in defense of teachers' rights.

Since 1971 the voucher question, with the same wording, has been repeated from time to time in the Gallup Poll. According to a report on the polls in the September 1986 issue of the *Phi Delta Kappan*, the percentage of the general public in favor of vouchers reached a 51 percent majority in 1983, and slipped to forty-six percent in 1986. One reason for the gain since 1970 has been the change in opinion among minorities, especially blacks, who were originally concerned that vouchers might lead to private segregated schools—a legitimate concern. Gradually, however, they became aware that: (a) this is prohibited by law and could be specifically prohibited in any voucher-enabling legislation; and (b) that the public schools continue to remain de facto segregated anyway, with schools attended by minorities almost uniformly provided with fewer resources.

Thomas Sowell has said, in answer to the claim that parent choice would lead to schools segregated along income, class, and racial lines, that what we have now by all evidence is already a record of segregation. This realization was no doubt a contributing factor in altering the opinion among blacks and persuading them thereafter to register regular majorities for parent and student freedom of educational choice.

In February 1971 a new voice appeared, that of Stephen Arons, who has written incisively and brilliantly of both the need and the constitutional grounds for separation of school and state, which he views as more urgent and justified than separation of church and state. As a staff attorney for the Center for Law and Education at Harvard, he participated in the 1970 OEO *Educational Vouchers* study. His article, "Equity, Option and Vouchers" was published in the *Teacher College Record*. Then in 1983 his book *Compelling Belief* was published, a work that is highly recommended to anyone wishing to explore this issue more deeply.

Those heading the opposition included: The National Education Association, the American Federation of Teachers, the American Association of School Administrators, the National School Boards Association, the National Congress of Parents and Teachers, joined by the Baptist Joint Committee, the American Jewish Congress and the American Civil Liberties Union.

These mostly liberal, even militant groups, were ready at the drop of a slogan to vociferously advocate "freedom," "liberty," "individual rights," and support for "the people" with both rhetoric and action—only as long as rights did not include the right of parents to have a choice in the education of their children.

Why would such an organization as the national PTA ever oppose parents' rights? Anyone familiar with the organization knows that in the past it has often been more concerned with supporting the public-school system than with parents' rights.

The stronger unified opposition of the education organizations to vouchers in 1971 caused Gerald E. Stroufe, Executive Director of the National Committee for Support of the Public Schools to note with sadness that

[W]hile the voucher plan has offered despairing parents hope, the education organizations have chosen to attack the source of the hope rather than the causes of despair.

Reviewing Jencks's proposal, Stroufe held that

The special magic of education vouchers is that they offer hope to a society that increasingly doubts the capability of traditional education structures and methods for educating their children. (Stroufe 1971, 90)

The courts, meanwhile, continued to deal with the separation of church and state, and legislative attempts to provide vouchers for nonpublic schools only. Perhaps the most important single case in this regard was handed down June 28, 1971, *Lemon v. Kurtzman*, from Pennsylvania. The U.S. Supreme Court again ruled against such limited aid, because the nonpublic schools are predominantly denominational, and a majority of them are associated with just one church. Such aid is, therefore, likely to excessively and unconstitutionally involve government and religion.

Speaking for the Court, Chief Justice Warren Burger established a framework that has been cited innumerable times since, not least of all by the Court itself. He said prior Court decisions include three tests that determine whether the requirements of the First Amendment religious clause are met.

> First, the statute must have a secular legislative purpose; second, its principal or primary effect must be one that neither advances nor inhibits religion; finally, the statute must not foster "an excessive entanglement with religion." (612)

> Our prior holdings do not call for total separation between church and state; total separation is not possible in an absolute sense. Some relationship between government and religious organizations is inevitable. . . . Judicial caveats against entanglement must recognize that the line of separation, far from being a "wall," is a blurred, indistinct, and variable barrier depending on all the circumstances of a particular relationship. (614)

Associate Justice William O. Douglas, in a concurring opinion wrote:

> The government may, of course, finance a hospital though it is run by a religious order, provided it is open to people of all races and creeds. The government itself could enter the hospital business; and it would, of course, make no difference if its agents who ran its hospitals were Catholics, Methodists, agnostics, or what not. For the hospital is not indulging in religious

instruction or guidance or indoctrination. (633)

He noted:

> In 1960 the Federal Government provided $500 mil-
> lion to private colleges and universities. Amounts
> contributed by state and local governments to private
> schools at any level were negligible. Just one decade
> later federal aid to private colleges and universities
> had grown to $2.1 billion. State aid had begun and
> reached $100 million. . . . we are now reaching a point
> where state aid is being give to private elementary and
> secondary schools as well as colleges and universities.
> (630, fn.)

On the other side of the continent, the California Supreme
Court handed down the first of two decisions ruling that the
method of funding public education in that state was unconstitutional, that education is a "fundamental right." In a subsequent case from Texas, The U.S. Supreme Court later decided
that education is not such a right, at least not under the U.S.
Constitution.

The California decision, known subsequently as *Serrano I*,
remained in force under provisions of that state's own
constitution. When the matter was not corrected to that court's
satisfaction, it followed with *Serrano II*, in 1976, and even
specified remedies that would meet its test for fairness. One of
those remedies named by the court was the use of vouchers.

In Cuernavaca, Mexico, however, there were those associated with Ivan Illich, the "deschooling" activist, who thought
trying to deal with schooling problems through cumulative
change was a waste of time. One of these "deschoolers," Everett
Reimer, wrote:

> The only ways of making sure that poor children get
> their fair share of public funds for education are either
> to segregate them completely in schools of their own,
> or to give the money directly to them. The first of these
> alternatives has been tried and has conspicuously

failed. The second provides a key to the proper alloca-
tion of educational resources. (Reimer 1971, 12/6)

Reimer admitted this was not a panacea that would solve
all of the problems of education, but he still regarded it as an
essential part of any solution. Like others, he concluded that
voucher schools would stand or fall to the degree they did or
did not satisfy their clients.

Throughout the year, there were reports, studies, and
individual views calling for more funding of higher education
through the student rather than directly to the institution.
Though not concerned with elementary and secondary education, these recommendations are of more than passing interest.
For one thing, there have always been funds for student assistance at this level, whether from governments, corporations,
foundations, the colleges and universities themselves, individual benefactors, or other sources. For another, this has become
ever more common in the years since that time. Federal aid
alone has skyrocketed.

Most importantly, this approach has rarely been controversial. There may be debates over how much money is enough,
but virtually none over whether student aid is desirable, whether
it benefits the student, whether it encourages individual choice,
or whether it harms the institutions. The practice of student aid
certainly has benefitted and not destroyed the public sector in
higher education, yet some in the field of education predict
destruction of basic education if a voucher system is allowed.
A practice universally praised in one segment of the educational community is thus generally condemned by the professional leadership in the other.

It is difficult to understand why a seventeen- or eighteen-
year-old in college is judged worthy of support and capable of
making an independent decision, while a student of the same
age in high school is not. What about college students who are
even younger? For example, the author's daughter went to
college at *fifteen*, directly after her sophomore year in high
school—a practice now encouraged and supported by the state
of Minnesota.

As a matter of fact, hundreds of colleges and universities

no longer require a high school diploma for a student to be accepted, although this option is not generally known and, therefore, relatively few students take advantage of it.

Neal V. Sullivan, a leading public educator, while not endorsing a plan he considered unproven, was equally unwilling to condemn it, for the same reason.

> Where do I stand on this suggestion? I am willing to
> give it a chance under *carefully* controlled conditions
> on a pilot basis. (Sullivan 1971, 83)

George Pearson was confident there was no constitutional barrier, citing as evidence a number of Supreme Court cases that permitted government financial assistance to private education: *Quick Bear vs. Leupp, Everson vs. Board of Education,* and *Allen vs. Board of Education*—cases likewise cited in this book.

Pearson favored vouchers over tax credits because the latter are not as beneficial to the poor as to the affluent, and because of possible cash flow problems if credits were not usable at the time tuition was due. He regarded the argument that voucher-supported schools might be irresponsible, or otherwise inadequate, as not valid. States already place a number of restrictions upon nonpublic schools, such as requiring state approval, having minimum curriculum requirements, and even, as in Connecticut, requiring them to be nonprofit and to have open enrollment whereby any qualified student is admitted.

The concern over fly-by-night schools or educational scams also ignores the existence of the various accrediting and evaluation agencies, and associations representing private schools. Even without governmental regulation, which would certainly continue, these bodies rate schools and programs, a process most schools participate in on a voluntary basis because it gives them status and legitimacy. Schools with appropriate or superior recognition would not keep that a secret from students and parents.

David Friedman argued that, while the voucher system would not end class distinctions, it would blur them. Instead of a few going to exclusive prep-schools, the middle class having moderately good suburban schools, and the inner-city poor getting custodial schools, with a voucher system a greater degree of equalization would take place.

> (T)he voucher plan, like other free market mechanisms, provides the ultimate form of decentralization, and does so in a way that protects the rights of even small minorities. (Friedman, n.d., 7)

A partial voucher plan was supported by the Governor of Illinois and was passed by the House but not by the Senate. This defeat took place in a state where

> the public schools prefer not to deal with some children, such as the spastic child, and refuse to accept them. Since the law requires that schooling be made available to all children, these undesirable (undesirable to public schools) children are provided with vouchers equal to the tuition charged by the private school they choose to attend. (Brozen and Weil 1971, 6, fn.)

Many other states similarly pay most or all of the costs for educating certain special education children at nonpublic schools.

These authors also suggest that, rather than receive a voucher, parents might pay a school's tuition fee and be reimbursed later. An advantage of this approach is that the school might not know the family is receiving governmental assistance. The disadvantage, of course, is that they would have to come up with the money first, and millions of parents would not be able to do this.

The argument in the report of the Carnegie Commission on Higher Education, *Institutional Aid*, which favored more funding of students rather than institutions, might apply equally well to basic education.

> There is little chance that such grants would encourage colleges to excessive catering to the whims of

students. . . . Having enormous inertia, colleges and universities are hardly likely to go overboard. . . . But, since present funding patterns provide a negative incentive to campus authorities toward responsiveness and change, even a modest positive incentive is an improvement. (Carnegie Commission 1972, 128)

In its January 1971 issue, *The National Elementary Principal* reported the results of a poll of its membership on vouchers: forty-three percent indicated strong opposition, twenty-three percent thought it would divert public funds from public schools, fifteen percent favored it, and nineteen percent registered no opinion (99).

The next month Allan Ornstein had an article in the *Journal of Secondary Education* in which he said:

If it were not for the school system's monopoly on the education of the poor, the schools would have gone bankrupt long ago. As of now the population that can afford to send their children to private and parochial schools or flee to the suburbs do just that—and in doing so forsake the city public schools. (Ornstein 1971, 91)

Stephen Arons appeared in the *Teacher College Record* with one of the links in his carefully reasoned chain on the question of constitutionality, a chain leading to *Compelling Belief* twelve years later. He regarded it as at least arguable that vouchers would meet the First Amendment test. At the same time, he was doubtful of the plan's adoption because support for it depends upon a value system which he believes not many Americans hold. This value system would include a commitment to equality, real respect for a pluralistic society, and a high regard for individuals and children. Lacking that, it is hard to see a source of support for vouchers.

It is likely that were a voucher scheme adopted by the states tomorrow, it would reflect the same values which are presently aggravating the abominable situation of American education. (Arons 1971, 362)

He saw other problems, including the lack of a base of support, partially because the idea is an abstract one and because it seemed to still be a slogan without ownership. The primary need was to organize a force that would regard vouchers as being in its self-interest and that would adopt a strategy supporting the community and free school movement, the most dependable political base for vouchers.

> In any case, it will not be really clear whether or not the idea is beneficial until enough political forces have lined up to see who is in a position to fashion its design . . . like other revolutions, it does not matter so much who starts it as who gains control of it once it has begun. (Arons 1971, 363)

That is still true today, although interest in vouchers has continued to grow and, in mid-1988, representatives of interested organizations met in Washington exploring the possibility of forming a coalition.

In "The Economics of the Voucher System," Eli Ginzberg expressed great doubt that there might be enough people who would modify or create schools that would be more directed toward student needs and interests. He regarded such an assumption as simply unwarranted. He also concluded that the argument that vouchers would give the disadvantaged some power was a reason they would not be adopted.

> It is fatuous to believe that the white community will permit a voucher system to operate so as to remove the barriers that they have laboriously erected to protect themselves and their children from what they consider to be the undesirable behavior patterns of the disadvantaged. (Ginzberg 1971, 380)

As for the repeated argument that the family would be unable to know what is best for their children's education, Mary Jo Bane said that

> the present state of education indicates that their judgments can hardly be worse than those now made by

the professionals and the state. (Bane 1971, 82)

She also said of the NEA and AFT:

> their main objections seem to be ideological—that a
> voucher system would "destroy the public schools."
> They do not seem to have carefully considered the
> possibility that this might be a good thing. (Bane 1971,
> 80)

The old cliche that "where you stand depends on where
you sit," was exemplified by David Selden, a strong opponent
of tuition vouchers until he retired as president of the national
AFT. He then wrote an article, which was published in 1975,
"Vouchers: A Critic Changes His Mind," lauding the idea and
the impact it had on the community of Alum Rock.

An encouraging sign, well developed in the 1960s, before
vouchers became a hot issue, was that more and more classroom teachers were speaking out, challenging the system, and
proposing radical changes. Among this group were George
Dennison, James Herndon, John Holt, Herbert Kohl, and Jonathan Kozol.

The final report of a White House Conference on Youth
held in Washington in April 1971 recommended that educational vouchers be made available on an annual basis to any
school rated acceptable by an educational voucher agency
established for this purpose. It suggested performance contracting could be used as a transitional device to move from the
present system to vouchers.

The report expressed confidence that vouchers would lead
to a more diversified secondary school system, especially with
the inclusion of private vocational schools, which it also favored. Realizing such a change could not be rapidly achieved,
and that there are plenty of potential problems, the report
called for a pilot project for which an annual appropriation of
fifty million dollars should be made (53). The states, too, should
fund research and development, alternative programs and
materials, including deferred tuition, independent study, and
work-study programs, as well as vouchers and performance
contracting (87).

The May 1971 issue of *Phi Delta Kappan*, reported that thirty-seven percent of Kappans (forty-five percent of the teachers, twenty-nine percent of the administrators) favored the voucher plan as did forty-three percent of the public (512).

On June 28, 1971, the Supreme Court upheld the Higher Education Facilities Act of 1963, providing federal construction grants for college and university facilities other than

> any facility used or to be used for sectarian instruction or as a place for religious worship, or . . . primarily in connection with any part of the program of a school or department of divinity.

In other words, federal construction grants could go to private institutions of higher education except for facilities with a direct religious purpose.

The Court held there is less danger in higher education than in basic education that

> religion will permeate the area of secular education, since religious indoctrination is not a substantial purpose or activity of these church-related colleges . . .

but Associate Justice Byron White didn't agree with this distinction, arguing that if one could be aided so could the other. It is not unknown for minority opinions on the Court to ultimately become the majority view, even if it is a minority of one, as with *Plessy v. Ferguson* in 1896.

Charles Benson and Thomas A. Shannon added a response to the argument that the public-school system deserves support because of its beneficial effects.

> (T)he present system should not be defended on account of the benign way it distributes educational resources. It is not benign. (Benson and Shannon 1972, 50)

George LaNoue passed along the reminder that, in 1969, before the OEO project, a Gallup Poll showed fifty-nine percent of the respondents would take advantage of a voucher plan if it were available.

Thomas Sowell reminded everyone that both the theory and the practice of vouchers have an extensive past, especially in higher education. The source of the opposition to its more general application in basic education comes from those with vested interest in the status quo, as is to be expected (Sowell 1972, 243). Sowell speculated that not only would vouchers permit parents to make choices regarding their children's education but it would almost force them to do so, thus encouraging them to become better informed on the subject. Since there is no one best form of education a greater variety might arise. One set of parents might not choose one school for all their children but might select the appropriate system for each child (246-47). In the soon-to-be voucher project in Alum Rock, parents did exactly that.

Sowell particularly commended support of vouchers by ghetto parents who cannot presently obtain the education they desire for their children. The self-selection process would make it easier to separate those who want to learn from those who don't and enhance the school's authority (247).

As to the objection that there might be discrimination practices in voucher schools, Sowell points out that that is what we have in the present public system. How can vouchers disrupt a nonexistent system of integration. Furthermore, present laws against racial discrimination will remain as effective, or ineffective, as they are with the current mix of public and private schools (Sowell 1972, 247-48).

The voucher system has many of the strong points of other reform proposals. It would foster decentralization, choice, and accountability. It would also give parents of students in private schools an incentive to vote for, not against, government funding for education (244-45).

On May 15, 1972, the U.S. Supreme Court, in *Wisconsin v. Yoder*, exempted the Amish from compulsory school attendance until age sixteen, holding that:

> The State's claim that it is empowered . . . to extend the
> benefit of secondary education to children regardless

of the wishes of their parents cannot be sustained against a free exercise claim of the nature revealed by this record, for the Amish have introduced convincing evidence that accommodating their religious objections by foregoing one or two additional years of compulsory education will not impair the physical or mental health of the child, or result in an inability to be self-supporting or to discharge the duties and responsibilities of citizenship, or in any other way materially detract from the welfare of society.

If the Amish may be granted such an exemption, may not others ultimately claim the same rights under the same conditions?

A 1972 study of New York State's programs of financial support for private schools for handicapped children concluded that vouchers for handicapped children have a history extending as far back as 1848, 1851, and 1852, when the legislatures of Massachusetts, New York, and Pennsylvania appropriated funds to private schools for the education of mentally retarded children. Some state schools for the handicapped, and even some public schools, began as private schools (Weintraub 1981, 49-50).

The new idea is, therefore, an old idea.

7

1973-1974
Alum Rock Project Begins

The major development of this period was that the Alum Rock voucher project was underway. There were two interim evaluations after the first and second years of operation: one in 1973 and another in 1974.

The review of the first year provided a recap of the reasoning behind the project: the present system of public schooling is essentially socialistic—centralized, bureaucratic, and uniform, and with a small governing board whose decisions are binding on everyone. However, a voucher system is almost totally the reverse: a market system—decentralized, nonbureaucratic, and diverse. Under the voucher system educators become professional producers, and parents and children become the consumers, with all having a large degree of personal choice and a variety of options from which they may choose (Joel Levin 1973, 53-54).

The 1973 review also gave credit to the Alum Rock teachers, who were organized in two separate units: one was the local chapter of the National Education Association and the other was the local chapter of the American Federation of Teachers. Both chapters supported the demonstration project despite vitriolic opposition from their respective organizations at both the state and national levels (Joel Levin 1973, 5).

Most of the 1973 report was, of course, devoted to the first-year developments.

Levin found that the project had a profound effect upon the district, challenging former procedures, changing the district's culture, altering attitudes about evaluation, increasing parent involvement and generally affecting all aspects of the district's operation. Above all, it did bring about significant variations in the number and variety of educational programs that were available to the students, the anticipated result before the project began (Joel Levin 1973, 32).

At first, many voucher advocates were regarded with suspicion, or even as enemies of public education. However, as the year progressed and observers from all over the country visited the project, a reassessment took place and the subject became an acceptable subject for discussion (Joel Levin 1973, 38).

Teachers worked together in small groups to cooperatively plan and carry out programs. Each group represented a self-contained minischool. From a professional point of view, one important result was the increased sense of "ownership" experienced by the teachers, who could now develop and implement their own ideas.

While one of the conditions for the program was that no staff member would lose his or her job, teachers who were perceived as ineffective, as not carrying their share of the responsibilities, or as the cause of parents' avoiding a program were the object of the group's concern. Recognizing that they shared a responsibility for making the minischool work and that an unsuccessful program would lack students, teachers became much more sensitive to the inadequacies of their peers. The group's professional response to any such inadequacies was not a negative evaluation, or public embarrassment, but an attempt to help their colleagues improve (Joel Levin 1973, 33).

Another result of the Alum Rock project was the change in the role and relationships of teachers, principals, and central staff. Teachers showed much more interest in the process, took their responsibilities more seriously now that they had more authority as well, and showed more sensitivity to their peers since there was a greater degree of interrelationship in their activities.

Central staff members began to function less as line administrators and more as staff consultants. They were utilized more deliberately than before. In a typical school environment, school psychologists are freely available from the central office upon request and availability. In the voucher project this was still true, except that each minischool had its own budget allotment against which the use of central personnel was charged. They were now likely to be used more efficiently, called upon only when the minischool staff deemed the service to be specifically needed and desirable. In this way, at the school level, teachers had much more control over the expenditures of their educational dollars.

Principals maintained their ultimate responsibility for school operations but functioned more often as resource consultants to the faculty (Joel Levin 1973, 39); that is, they functioned more as counselors and advisors, and less as authority figures, a distinction that increased rather than decreased their importance. Principals elsewhere should find this reassuring.

Both voucher advocates and opponents had one surprise. The prediction that there would be sweeping changes if the power of the purse was given to parents through a voucher mechanism was proven wrong. There was no chaos, no segregation in the schools, and no brutal competition. Nor did parents try to bring about radical changes in the schools (Joel Levin 1973, 53).

In general they took more interest in their children's education, which was an improvement over the more widespread parent apathy so often bemoaned in the typical school environment. Yet parents were often very explicit in indicating they did not want to make final decisions at the school level; that this was the job of professional educators. Parents were quite willing to allow the educators to decide which programs were presented as long as they could decide which they would choose for their children (Joel Levin 1973, 38).

It was encouraging that the growth of teacher independence and professionalism was accompanied in this way by a more active role for parents. Not only did parents have a right to choose from a variety of educational offerings, a right they exercised, but they also took part in screening new staff members for both the school district and individual schools. The increased activity by parents was also a distinct contrast to the view of voucher critics who said parents would be unable or unwilling to make knowledgeable decisions regarding their children's education.

So much for apathy, chaos, segregation, and other harmful results predicted by voucher opponents. Even though the voucher project had so many conditions that some question whether it should be regarded as a voucher experiment, students, parents, teachers, and administrators all seemed to benefit from the innovations.

In the present system parents have a lot to be apathetic about. Anyone who has sought permission from public school authorities for a change in decisions regarding a student, such as a change of teachers or schools, even within the same school district, knows how difficult that is. Change requires more political clout, or the expenditure of more time and energy, than a typical parent possesses.

Apathy decreases when individuals are given meaningful roles. Without such a role, and faced with resources overwhelmingly superior to those which the individual has available, apathy may well be a rational response.

The second year interim report was again positive. Among the changes receiving credit were: curriculum planning and design, and determination of resource allocations by classroom teachers; the institutionalization of alternative education; the development of a budgeting system whereby educational dollars follow the child; the evolution of the principal's role to that of consultant and facilitator; the response of programs to a parental demand, including the phase-out of programs with insufficient interest; distribution to parents of program evaluation reports; parental and student choice of the educational style they prefer; and the involvement of the vast majority of teachers in programs which they designed consistent with their philosophy, and about which they are enthusiastic (Joel Levin 1974, 201).

Levin regarded teacher enthusiasm and commitment as "Perhaps the most striking outcome of the project." Because of the feeling of ownership and responsibility which they developed for the programs they designed, they came to have a vested interest and professional pride in making them successful. On their own, they worked longer hours and extra days seeking to improve their minischools. Peer pressure was mobilized where it was felt that a member was not doing his or her share. Just as Adam Smith had predicted (Joel Levin 1974, 202, 204).

The net result was significant change in a large, complex system. In short, the hopes of voucher advocates seemed to have more justification than the fears of voucher opponents.

Evan Jenkins was quoted by *Phi Delta Kappan* as saying the experiment rated an "A" because of less absenteeism and vandalism, greater educational variety, and more enthusiasm for school (*Phi Delta Kappan*, Sept. 1973, 77).

A summary of parent and teacher opinions in the general press reported:

> 95% of the parents said they like having a choice of schools for their children; 75% felt their children will get a better education this way... 96% of the teachers said there was more opportunity to be innovative ... 2/3 thought parents should have more say about what their children learn in school; and 2/3 thought vouchers would help do this (Lofton 1974).

There may not be another school district in the nation that could produce similar results.

It might be concluded that such findings would lead to a more general adoption of this approach, even though it was not a general voucher project in which any student could go to any public or nonpublic school, in or out of the district. But this has not happened. What occurred in Alum Rock was not widely disseminated to the general public, and hardly reported at all by the educational organizations to their members.

Establishment opposition to the project remained throughout its existence, and continues to this day. Despite what many would view as successes in Alum Rock, the pessimistic view of

Neil Postman and Charles Weingartner in 1973, that "pressures against the voucher system, including the force of institutional inertia, will prevail" has been correct (Postman and Weingartner 1973,196-97).

Nationally, educators still complain about direction from above; government rules, regulations, and restrictions; and political interference. They do not realize that political involvement goes with the territory in the present arrangement, and will persist as long as the current system continues.

What Richard M. Cyert, president of Carnegie-Mellon University in Pittsburgh wrote in 1974 in support of funding higher education through the students has relevance for basic education:

> (T)hrough this system, public institutions could escape the political influences of state legislatures... The legislature can effectively transfer its concerns over curricula and similar matters to the control stemming from students' free choice... Students... will do better choosing for themselves than by having others choose for them (Cyert 1974, 9).

It also would have a tendency to equalize the resources available to students. Many opponents of vouchers cite the possibility (or, as some claim, the likelihood) that students would be segregated by wealth and social class, even if not directly by race. They direct their rhetoric at the nonpublic schools as evidence, ignoring the fact that those schools, as a category, have about half the per-pupil resources of the public schools and that their student body is not composed of an elite.

They should look, instead, at the public system. When allusions are made to that system as a great leveller, the reference is often to national figures. If you look at the more than fifteen thousand school districts, with about forty million students, of course you have a composite of America. It is not, however, a composite that most students experience. They do not attend a national system or a school district. Rather, they are enrolled at a particular school where they are assigned to specific classes, relatively few of which have anything modestly resembling the "melting pot" so often alluded to in literature about public schooling.

As Daniel J. Sullivan pointed out in 1974, in a school district there may be any number of students from ten to one million—a ratio that from one extreme to the other might be greater than one hundred thousand to one. At the same time in terms of per-pupil expenditures the range was from less than $200 to more than $14,000 per student—a ratio greater than seventy to one. These are calculations based on districts, but since districts do not always spend the same amount per pupil in each of their schools, there could be an even greater differential among America's eighty-seven thousand public school buildings. These statistics come as no surprise to Americans who are aware of the reality that a student elite exists in the nation's public schools (Sullivan 1974, 75). One way this elitism is achieved is through tax breaks for the wealthy.

Tuition tax credits have been advocated for the support of nonpublic schools. Not only is this proposal not as advantageous for the general public as vouchers but also the debate over it fails to recognize its similarity to the property tax as a support for schools.

The tuition tax credit would be available to those who pay taxes (though some have advocated a "negative" credit, with a reimbursement to those too poor to pay an income tax). In its simple form, therefore, its advantage is to those who pay income taxes, proportional to income, up to the limit of the credits.

The property tax deductible from the federal income tax return is a similar benefit for homeowners, with a much higher upper limit than those proposed for tax credits, but of no use to renters.

Generally speaking, the wealthier the individual, the more valuable the personal home(s), the higher the property tax, the greater the tax deduction, and, because of the graduated income tax, the greater the tax savings.

As a result, wealthy individuals who desire advantageous schooling for their children do not need to send them to private schools, and most of them do not. All they need do is live together in an exclusive community, as most of them do, base their support for their school district on the property tax, and deduct those taxes from their income.

This is all constitutional and proper. In this democratic society, anyone who can afford an expensive home can have a public school of choice. All that is needed is to move into the right community. With more land per home, smaller families, and fewer students per square mile than the common folk, a per-pupil expense of $5,000 or more (based on the 1974 economy) is easily possible.

Higher education continued to provide its share of voucher rationales. From 1947 to 1973, 8 commissions studying higher education supported the proposition that "Federal financial assistance for higher education should be granted primarily through students rather than through institutions." Three supported it strongly, five, moderately. A ninth commission opposed it (Carnegie Commission on Higher Education, *Priorities for Action*, 1973, 172).

An example of the implementation of these recommendations was the passage of the Basic Educational Opportunity Grant Program in 1972, which provides funding directly to the student.

Norwood v. Harrison, decided by the Supreme Court on June 25, 1973, with the majority opinion written by Chief Justice Warren Burger, provided further contrary evidence to those critics who suggested vouchers would lead to greater racial discrimination and segregation. The Court ruled that Mississippi could not give textbooks to students at private schools excluding blacks.

John Holt, himself a teacher and the author of several books about, and critical of, public schooling, said educational coercion is no assurance of success. The government cannot possibly guarantee that providers of such services will be kind, competent, and unselfish. With a captive clientele the odds favor just the reverse, as repeated examples from various kinds of public institutions have demonstrated all too frequently. The remedy is to give to everyone the right to decide how they will be helped.

Given any real choice and alternatives almost everyone will manage his life better than anyone else,
however expert, could manage it for him. (Holt 1974,
85)

James D. Koerner said the present system condemns everyone

to a twelve-year ride . . . Suggestions for improving the
ride and alleviating the confusion are constantly well-
ing up from the passengers. On occasion there is even
a radical proposal for abandoning the bus altogether
and letting everyone decide on his own destination
and means of reaching it; but such proposals are
invariably denounced as demagogic or simply chi-
merical (Koerner 1974, 178).

What he would like to see are fundamental changes featur-
ing choice that would increase the options from the present
zero level (Koerner 1974, 179).

In England, Michael Huberman had something to say
about credentials and certificates when he suggested vouchers

would send teachers, along with other certified specialists or professionals, into the educational marketplace. Theoretically, teachers could advertise their
special training and skill at adapting learning tasks to
different ages and abilities.

Huberman also noted that there is research suggesting that
untrained housewives can be as effective as trained teachers in
some educational roles (Huberman 1974, 54-55).

In Denmark a group of families which starts a school and
keeps it operating for a year becomes eligible for national
support of eighty-five percent of the school's operating costs.
Capital costs remain the obligation of the supporting families.

This is just one of many variations by which other democracies have found ways to support family choice in education—
and remain democracies. Only dictatorships, or societies

doubting the soundness of their values, must compel the young to undergo years of state indoctrination in how and what to think.

Robert M. Healey, writing of educational practices in France that include private school aid, summarized federal programs doing the same in the States, the Reserve Officers Training Corps, ROTC; the National School Lunch Act of 1946; Title IV of the Housing Act of 1950, which authorized long-term low-interest loans to provide housing and other educational facilities at public or private educational institutions offering at least a two-year program leading to a bachelor's degree; and the National Defense Education Act of 1958, which makes loans to both public and private elementary and secondary schools.

Even more directly related to the voucher question is the Elementary and Secondary Education Act of 1965. Its Title I makes federal funds to local school boards also available to furnish educational services to private and parochial school pupils. Under Title II, textbooks may be purchased for loan to students attending private and parochial schools (Healey 1974, 41-42). Since Healey's publication, additional programs have been introduced at both the state and local levels.

In 1974, a Teachers National Field Task Force reported to HEW that vouchers may be justified to provide educational alternatives to students and parents. "If this should provide a better education and more satisfactory working conditions, it is worthy of further investigation" (*Inside-Out* 1974, 40).

A Ford Foundation report concluded:

> Although no Constitutional barrier exists to spending public funds on private nonsectarian schools, legislative and political inhibitions usually prevent such expenditures. (*Matters of Choice* 1974, 4)

David L. Kirp and Mark G. Yudof in *Educational Policy and the Law* noted the lack of a constitutional barrier to nonsectarian school aid:

> Several states have adopted voucher schemes that enable handicapped youngsters, whose educational needs cannot be adequately met by the public school

system, to attend state-regulated private schools. (Kirp and Yudof 1974, 710)

If regular students cannot be provided for at the expense of the handicapped, can the handicapped receive benefits denied to regular students?

Virgil Blum reminded his listeners that

> The child benefit rule of law is the legal basis of scores of state and federal tuition-grant programs, all of which permit the grant recipient to go to church-related schools. There are more than 100 college tuition-grant laws in 39 states. Millions of grants are given to college students under the GI Bill of Rights, the National Defense Education Act, the Federal Basic Educational Opportunity Program, and the Supplementary Opportunity Program. (Blum 1974, 339)

George Maddox suggested a general application of vouchers:

> We are still uncertain about how to finance the Learning Society . . . there is clearly a growing interest in a voucher system financed in part by public money which would permit individuals to consider investing in a variety of learning and educational programs at various points in the life cycle. (Maddox 1974, 23)

The Citizens for Educational Freedom, a parent organization, celebrated its fifteenth anniversary in 1974 by endorsing vouchers and holding a day-long symposium in St. Louis on the subject. One of the presenters at the symposium was columnist and commentator M. Stanton Evans who told those present

> the principle objective is to achieve . . . the secular purpose of better public and private education in America . . . to have some chance of getting the voucher system adopted either at the state or federal level it is necessary to put together a comprehensive coalition of people, all of whom have different motives but similar

objectives and all of which can be encompassed by an intelligent voucher scheme. *(Educational vouchers— symposium views)*

That comprehensive coalition awaited creation. An attempt was to begin in mid-1988.

8

1975-1976
Theory and a Model

One of the strongest arguments in support of family choice in education is that only in this manner will the ongoing struggle for control be ended. In 1975 R. J. Lytle pointed out the frustrations in the ongoing system:

> the only way one group of parents can have their curriculum or schedule proposals adopted is at the expense and dissatisfaction of another group of parents. . . . So the normal situation is a constant war between competing groups. (Lytle 1975, 9)

This argument for family choice has grown stronger over the years along with other arguments for individual rights in and out of schools.

For example, teachers, parents, students, and others continue to battle over whether or not sex education should be part of the school curriculum. But isn't that a value judgment that will never be reconciled to everyone's satisfaction? No program a school district offers can ever satisfy all viewpoints. Neither can the decision not to offer a program.

If a majority did exist for offering such a course, there would still be a minority that would be opposed to, if not appalled by, the idea. Even the majority itself might be fragmented when it came to deciding the course content. For example:

what teacher should present it?
what textbook should be used?
what visual aids or supplemental materials should be
    used?
should a discussion of birth-control options be included?
should the material be presented within a moral frame-
    work of right or wrong? Or
should it be presented as a neutral presentation of the
    "facts" ?

Each viewpoint may be right for someone; and wrong for someone else. A one-system approach will never solve this dilemma. It would be unsettling enough if this were the only such question, but of course it isn't. It is but one of a long, and growing, list of divisive subjects which can never be resolved by any one locked-in-step school.

Why shouldn't educational issues be matters for parents to decide? Why should I have to tell you how your children will be educated in order for mine to be so treated, or you to tell me? Why should not both of us, and all other parents, decide individually and personally—at least to a far greater degree than we do now.

And not just parents. Why not involve the students in this decision-making process? The strongest case can be made for the eighteen-year-olds who may vote for president of the United States, or other public officials; may join the armed services and defend their country, at possibly a very high price; may decide health questions affecting them that can be literally matters of life or death; may, in many parts of the country, use alcohol legally; but in the present system, they may not decide what teacher(s) they want, what school they will attend (unless they have adequate personal funds), or what educational experiences they wish to have.

This is not to exclude younger students from the same process of choice. Most children of school age would be capable of expressing particular aspirations, needs, or interests that would help their parents in selecting a suitable school. People with funds who resort to private institutions make this kind of choice. Why not have this openness available to all students?

In the period 1975-76, surveys were taken of students on the question of a voucher system. Although adults, according to earlier Gallup Polls, had been divided on the voucher issue, the high school juniors and seniors surveyed were in favor of the idea by more than two to one (Jones and Jones 1976, 111). Two to one. No president has ever been elected by such a margin.

What are the impediments to a voucher system? There is one answer, which Don Davies of the Institute for Responsive Education, Boston University expressed:

> The elitist version of democracy has firm control of the hearts and minds of most Americans. We have been taught that ordinary people cannot be trusted to make decisions about complex matters in a large, technologically sophisticated society because they can't understand the consequences of their decisions ... We depend on experts and professionals. (Sandow and Apker 1975, 33)

If not many, at least some, opponents in the educational community were coming around. One was David Selden, a former president of the American Federation of Teachers:

> Kids like them, teachers like them, parents like them— even I've come to like the vouchers in Alum Rock. . . . When I last visited Alum Rock . . . the students all seemed to be involved in some activity in which they were genuinely interested. . . . Underlying it all, however, was a shared confidence that something different—and good—really was going on. (Selden 1975, 44-45)

Half of the district's twenty-eight elementary schools (it had no high schools) took part in the project, and each developed two to five minischools.

Noting that one national teacher leader used the first-year test scores to call the project a failure, Selden chided his former colleague, reminding him that teachers had objected for years to having themselves and their schools judged on the basis of pupil test scores. He objected to altering that stand to take some "cheap shots" at a good program. Among the project's best features, in Selden's judgment, was its emphasis on teacher control, diversity, and good community relations (Selden 1975, 46).

It is said, Better late than never. Perhaps, but not by much in Selden's case. By the time he came to appreciate the positive value in a voucher system, he was no longer AFT president, and not in a position to explain his change of heart to his hundreds of thousands of members, or again go to Congress representing his organization to recant his previous testimony. Even the issue of the magazine which presented his better judgment was its last.

Perhaps, like many leaders, he had thoughts along this line earlier, but didn't express them for organizational reasons, thinking his members would not be receptive—or at least those who decide the elections would not be. Whatever the reason, it is unfortunate that he did not speak out earlier.

> For years, the unions have demanded recognition of teaching as a full profession.... The irony: Only under a voucher plan would teachers be as "professional" as are doctors or lawyers. Professionals, except teachers, already work in an open marketplace. . . . With a voucher plan schools and teachers would be exposed to this kind of healthy competition. (Jones and Jones 1976, 112)

Occasionally there were educational leaders willing to consider criticism of the regular system. One instance came when the Pennsylvania State Education Association, under the leadership of President Joseph D'Andrea and Past-President Edward Smith, sponsored an educational conference, to which they invited distinguished speakers to tell it as they saw it.

> All of us here have been victimized by a structure that
> classified human beings. . . . This is a structure that
> labeled as "losers" such people as: Sir Isaac Newton,
> inattentive and a bad scholar; James Watt, dull and
> inept; Charles Darwin, rather below the common stan-
> dard in intellect; Thomas Edison, at the bottom of his
> class; Albert Einstein, mentally slow; Louis Pasteur,
> learned slowly; Carl Jung, poor mathematician; John
> Keats, no evidence of unusual ability; Yeats, poor
> student; Winston Churchill, backward, bottom of class;
> Abraham Lincoln and Henry Ford, showed no prom-
> ise; Edgar Allan Poe, expelled from school; Franklin
> Roosevelt, undistinguished at school; Nehru, ordi-
> nary. (Mario Fantini, *PSEA Bicentennial Symposium on
> Education*, 1976, 9-10)

These two leaders were notable in their efforts to promote
innovative ideas in the education community, but under association rules at that time, their leadership roles were restricted
to one year in office as president (preceded by one year as presi-
dent-elect and succeeded by one year as past-president). So
they soon left office and subsequent leaders, despite other
laudable qualities, have been much more conservative on
educational matters and not prepared to present controversial
topics.

During this period Stephen Arons questioned the wisdom
and the possible constitutionality of the state mandating the
schooling most children will receive.

He argues that the state cannot require parents to give up
their First Amendment rights in order for their children to
obtain a "free" education in the public schools, yet this is what
happens through the unavoidable majority control of those
schools. The majority, or at least ruling, view may well be
unacceptable to many. Those in such a situation apparently
have but two choices, either accept the "free" education at the
cost of their personal values or preserve their value system at

the sacrifice of the financial assistance others are receiving. But these may not be the only options since, "Conditioning the provision of government benefits upon the sacrifice of fundamental rights has been held unconstitutional before" (Arons 1976, 100).

Two of the court cases during this period are of particular interest. The first, in 1975, *Wood v. Strickland,* handed down by the U.S. Supreme Court, held that school officials may be liable for money damages, under federal law. While the decision awarded no such damages, the precedent was set for future use. This occurred in late 1986 when parents were awarded a substantial sum because their children were exposed to compulsory education to which they objected. The losing officials planned to appeal. Even if they win, however, the dangers to them under a compulsory system are growing.

Also in 1975 California Governor Jerry Brown signed into law a voucher driver education bill (*Legislative Review*, October 6, 1975, 2).

Finally, at the very end of this period, on Dec. 30, 1976, the California Supreme Court, in what became known as *Serrano II,* (*Serrano I* was handed down in 1971), again rejected that state's public school financing system, even though it was modified from what had existed at the time of the first decision. Expressing its objection, based on the state's constitution, to the validity of what had been achieved, the court went further and suggested options that would meet the requirements of the basic document. One of these was the use of vouchers, by themselves or in combination with other approaches.

It argued as follows:

> There exist several alternative potential methods of financing the public school system of this state which would not produce wealth-related spending disparities. These alternative methods, which are "workable, practical and feasible," include: (1) full state funding, with the imposition of a statewide property tax; (2) consolidation of the present 1,067 school districts into about five hundred districts, with

boundary realignments to equalize assessed valuations of real property among all school districts; (3) retention of the present school district boundaries but the removal of commercial and industrial property from local taxation for school purposes and taxation of such property at the state level; (4) [equalization of] school district power . . .; (5) vouchers; and (6) some combination of two or more of the above. (*California Supreme Court*, 557 PAC 929, 938)

For the first time, a court specifically stated that vouchers would be constitutional, if they were available for the general population. Not everyone was convinced, or wanted to be, and the U.S. Supreme Court had yet to speak on a broad-based voucher, but another step forward had been taken.

While the United States Supreme Court has rejected aid to religious schools on the constitutional grounds it conflicts with the First and Fourteenth Amendments, all of the cases involved have contained the same flaw: they sought to give aid only to nonpublic school students and their parents, which is quite a different question from giving such aid to all students and their parents.

As for vouchers causing the "better" students to flee, leaving the public school as the "schools of last resort," or "dumping grounds," (an expression that says something about its users attitude toward many public school students), this is most unlikely. The present nonpublic schools are not elitist, despite the undocumented claims of some in the public-school establishment. They include students of virtually every type, and often educate them more effectively than the public schools. It is highly unlikely, therefore, that virtually all students will not be welcomed somewhere. As for real juvenile delinquents, they "are a problem for the courts, not schools" (Lytle 1975, 25).

The disadvantages of government schools may well outweigh the advantages.

We consider our nation's economic system as being founded on free enterprise. . . . Why, then, the anomaly

of government control over education, which controls
the productive lives of nearly one third of the population? (Lytle 1975, 53-54)

In 1975 Milton Friedman returned to the fray (although he
really never left it). He felt, as did Stephen Arons, that the
compulsion of the public schools was the real violation of the
spirit of the First Amendment. In a somewhat more novel vein,
he suggested that vouchers might reduce the role of the parochial schools. Most nonpublic schools, after all, require some
form of subsidization in order to exist, and it is for that reason
that the great majority of them are affiliated with some religious
body that can support them with funds, low-paid staff, volun-
teers, tax-free status, and other aid.

With the use of vouchers these advantages would not
disappear but they would be less significant, and more nonpublic, nonparochial schools could survive on the tuition income
the vouchers would make possible (Friedman 1975, 275).

Public school advocates who think vouchers would not
only destroy the public system but enable the parochial system
to blossom might well be wrong on both counts. As would
those who might favor those outcomes.

As for the further fear that vouchers would encourage
social, class, and ideological insularity, Friedman agreed with
the view that this condition already exists in the public system.
Reports of prestigious public schools usually refer to such communities as Scarsdale, Lake Forest, or Beverly Hills. Such
stories are rarely accompanied by information that these are
among the highest personal income districts in the nation. They
are not blue collar, "melting pot" school districts with limited,
or even average, per capita wealth. They could be better described, in Friedman's view, as private tax shelters rather than
public schools. If they were really private, supported by direct
tuition fees paid by the community's wealthy citizens rather
than by property taxes, those costs would not be deductible
against federal income taxes (Friedman 1975, 278).

He also expressed "great sympathy" for compensatory
vouchers, such as proposed by Christopher Jencks. But he was

still inclined to favor his own earlier support for a standard voucher value because the politics of the matter would pervert the compensatory approach. While a standard voucher might be second-place to a compensatory one in an ideal world, it would stand a greater chance of being adopted and would still be superior to the present arrangement (Friedman 1975, 279).

A standard voucher would give the poor something they do not have currently, and that is choice.

As with many other advocates, he believes the very poor would benefit most. Friedman not only dismisses the arguments that the poor lack interest in their children, and competence to choose, as a "gratuitous insult," but says the nation's history gives more than adequate proof of how much people of limited means and advantages will sacrifice for their children when there is any hope the sacrifice will achieve results (Friedman 1975, 280).

He has given talks on the voucher plan from time to time, and has been greatly impressed with the number of those who afterward tell him that they have always wanted to teach or run their own school but were turned off by the rigidity and bureaucracy in the public schools where the great majority of the nation's youngsters are (Friedman 1975, 281).

As a teacher-advocate of this plan in the past, the author has had the same experience, even with teachers who took part in the 1970 NEA convention that condemned vouchers. There is no question but that many public school teachers would participate, and benefit, if vouchers were commonly adopted. Many others might remain in, return to, or enter, the field.

A 1975 report of a national survey of male high school seniors indicated what those sampled thought of their public schools.

> 6 percent rated their courses as "very exciting and stimulating." Only a third felt that they were learning "useful things" that would help them later in life. More than half said "the school doesn't offer the courses I want to take." Studies by the U.S. Department of Labor show that 70 percent of high school

dropouts, 78 percent of correctional institution in-
mates and 88 percent of the enrollees in manpower
training programs were in "general curriculum" school
programs that prepared them for neither college nor
careers. (Berenger 1975, 5)

A summary of Carnegie Commission on Higher Education
projects suggested that

Higher Education can be dragged into a new era
kicking and screaming by the budget, as would be the
case if public support were to be channeled through
students. (*Sponsored Research* 1975, 148)

Would not the same be true for basic education? David Melton,
a critic of public schooling, was not optimistic of the chances for
change:

The voucher plan is interesting, indeed, but it will
probably be doomed to die a slow death in bureaucratic red tape. (Melton 1975, 152)

Motivation for change in the public interest is another
difficulty. According to Thomas F. Green:

Anything that is viewed by some as in the general
interests of all, must sooner or later be translated into
something in the individual interests of certain specific individuals. Otherwise, what is good for the
society as a whole will not get done. (Sandow and
Apker 1975, 7)

Charles Benson and Thomas A. Shannon commented on
two major proposals for structural change in public education:

One of these radical solutions—full state funding—is
centralist. The other—family power equalizing—is
decentralist in the extreme. This proposal would use

vouchers to place decisions about resource allocations for education directly in the hands of households. (Benson and Shannon 1972, 41)

Friedrich A. von Hayek, winner of the 1974 Nobel Prize in Economic Science, emphasized the inflexibility of a socialistic educational environment.

If education is completely regulated by government you have excluded a great deal of the evolution of educational development and exploration. (Hayek 1975, 10)

A 1975 Supreme Court decision reviewing a Pennsylvania law held that most of the law was unconstitutional. Those who did not carefully read it assumed it was another indication that a general voucher plan would fail to meet the First Amendment test. What the Court said, however, was that

The specified aid to nonpublic schools, except for the loan of textbooks, is unconstitutional. Textbook loans are constitutional because they are the same for all children and the financial benefit is to parents and children, not to schools. (*Meek v. Pittenger* 421 U.S. 349, May 19, 1975)

Again, assistance to all children is acceptable.

Herbert Kiesling suggested that it wasn't necessary to go all the way to a voucher plan to open up the present system. The creation of a number of alternative public schools was already introducing the idea of client choice.

If these systems took one further step—directly or indirectly rewarding school personnel on the basis of how many students choose their schools—this would introduce into education the operation of a market mechanism similar to the competition of buyers in the private sector of the economy. (Kiesling 1975, 16)

Some school districts have since opted for open-enroll-ment plans with some limitations, such as acceptance on a space-available basis only and the choice being one of schools, not of teachers. This way all teachers have students assigned to them and no teacher faces the possible embarrassment of very few or no students choosing them.

On June 2, 1975, Pennsylvania state Senator John Sweeney, from Delaware County in suburban Philadelphia, told his colleagues,

> In my judgment each child who attends an accredited elementary or secondary school in this Common-wealth or any place in this Nation, public or private, is entitled to participate equally in the distribution of the available tax dollars raised for educational purposes. No child should be considered more equal or less equal than another child simply because of the accred-ited school that he or she attends . . . The Servicemen's Readjustment Act of 1944, as amended and adjudi-cated, established that there is no separation of church and State conflict in permitting public money to follow the student to the school of his or her choice. (*Legisla-tive Journal*—Senate, Pennsylvania, 345)

Although Pennsylvania is a state that has tried in various ways to assist its nonpublic schools—*Lemon v. Kurtzman* and *Meek v. Pittenger* were two Supreme Court decisions that arose because of that state's legislative enactments—no general voucher has yet been passed there. Sweeney himself later decided not to seek reelection to the Senate.

Efforts to find other school districts willing to try the idea failed. In Gary, Indiana, the teachers' organization killed it during contract negotiations. Rochester, New York, found both teacher opposition and disinterested parents, at a time it also was working toward desegregation. San Francisco and New Rochelle, New York, decided not to participate. This despite the fact that the then Secretary of Health, Education, and Welfare, Caspar W. Weinberger, had "a special interest in the notion" (Reinhold, 1975).

In East Hartford, Connecticut, the school board

voted 6-2 not to adopt . . . the proposed voucher system, which was to have been an extension of the open enrollment program, in effect since 1969. According to Andrew Esposito, coordinator of the Parents' Choice staff, "We're just not ready for it. Maybe in another two or three years we would have been, but not now." The town's 18 principals had voted unanimously against the proposal. (*Compact* 1976, 11)

Of course, "two or three years" later nothing happened.

Although not a participant in the federal government's search, I obtained several copies of the Jencks's proposal to the OEO and, in the early 1970s, discussed it with John C. Pittenger, Pennsylvania's Secretary of Education. It is his name, because of his position, that is on the Supreme Court case already mentioned. Following these meetings, we met with the superintendent and board of education in Harrisburg, Pennsylvania, to see if they would be interested in participating in a pilot project.

One of the advantages of using this district for any model program is that Harrisburg is the state capital and is visited annually by thousands of educators, school board members, and others from around the state for various purposes. They would therefore be able to see a demonstration there without the necessity for additional trips or costs.

District officials did take the question seriously. A number read the Jencks proposal, and there was a degree of interest in making such an effort. However, like Rochester, the district was involved in a desegregation plan. It called for changing the two city high schools to one for grades nine and ten and one for grades eleven and twelve, with cross-district busing so all students would attend both schools. The conclusion was that this would involve enough controversy without trying to get a voucher proposal adopted at the same time. In all fairness, that seemed to be a reasonable decision.

Still, positive support and studies continued to appear.

The Kettering Commission proposed federal aid and state legislation that would entitle every citizen to fourteen years of tuition-free education, only eight of which would be compulsory. The remaining six years would be available to the individual for use at any stage of his life. (Passow 1976, 44)

The Committee on Economic Development, a leading business study group saw a broader application of the idea.

The monopolistic character of most public-service agencies is one reason for their lack of interest in productivity. One way of responding to this situation is to encourage competition and consumer choice . . . Competition can be enhanced by supplying consumers with vouchers or other forms of purchasing power and permitting them to select services from private or public suppliers. (CED, 1976, 22)

Stephen Arons further developed his thesis regarding school and state. The efficacy of modest changes did not impress him.

A First Amendment reading of *Pierce* suggests, therefore, that the present state system of compulsory attendance and financing of public schools does not adequately satisfy the principle of government neutrality toward family choice in education. (Arons 1976, 78)

In an article in the February 1976 issue of the *Harvard Educational Review*, he reminded his readers of Ivan Illich's observation: "The school has become the established church of secular times" (Arons 1976, 104).

Newsweek reported in early 1976:

Thirty-four states have recently adopted "voucher" systems that supply college aid to individual students, who can use it at schools of their choice. (*Newsweek*, April 26, 1976, 63)

Is there really that great a distinction between basic and postsecondary education? Should there be?

Two months later, the U.S. Supreme Court again

supported governmental regulation of private schools operating in an unfair or discriminatory fashion.

> Section 1981 prohibits private, commercially oper-ated, nonsectarian schools from denying admission to prospective students because they are Negroes . . . While parents have a constitutional right to send their children to private schools and to select private schools that offer specialized instruction, they have no consti-tutional right to provide their children with private school education unfettered by reasonable govern-ment regulation. (*Runyon v. McCrary*, 161)

Syndicated columnist Sydney Harris was more optimistic (assuming you favor vouchers) than some.

> It's probable that before this century is over, the public school system in the U.S. will be abandoned, replaced by competing private schools for which parents will be given "vouchers" by the government to pay for their children's education. (Harris 1976, 14)

Thomas Sowell countered the claim that the poor are not sufficiently interested in the welfare of their children to do anything about it:

> It is not uncommon today for the bulk of the student body in these (Catholic) schools to be non-Catholic. Some . . . have achieved remarkable educational suc-cess with black students, at far lower cost per pupil than the public schools. . . . If educational vouchers were to make education free at both private and public institutions, would black parents be too helpless to make a choice among various schools available to them? Or is the real problem that many caretakers in the educational bureaucracies would find themselves out of a job? (Sowell 1976, 2)

Theodore Sizer issued a reminder that "The common school, the single institution built around a common American creed, never was and clearly will never be" (Sizer and Sizer 1976, 34).

John Coons, a leading advocate of vouchers is also one of the relatively few who early on believed that this would be to the advantage of teachers.

> Families with the new option to change schools would seldom ignore the counsel of the child's present teacher or counselor . . . This new equality in the relationship should increase, not diminish, respect for the counsel of the educator. (Coons 1976, 23)

U.S. News & World Report remarked on the ongoing success of the GI Bill which, in the thirty years since the end of World War II had provided benefits for nearly seventeen million veterans (September 6, 1976, 69).

And there were additional judgments on the Alum Rock project, now ending.

Mary Ganz found pros and cons, with over fifty mini-schools, each created by groups of four or five teachers voluntarily working together, using many different teaching styles. There were three or four such minischools in each of the fourteen participating school buildings, half the district's total. (Ganz 1976, 4)

Still, Richard Reyes, who was in charge of evaluating the project for the district, said it wasn't a real test of vouchers, despite all the options and the high degree of decentralization. And, while by the fourth year of the program (the 1975-76 school year), nearly thirty percent of the parents in the experiment were having their children bused to schools outside of their neighborhoods to take advantage of different minischools, few parents were taking an active role in running the schools (Ganz 1976, 4).

While a disappointment to those hoping to see such parent activity, or control, this last point could be viewed as a positive development by those who were concerned over a possible further dilution of what little autonomy teachers normally have in a public school environment.

Despite the opposition of their national affiliates to the project,

Alum Rock teachers have used the minischools' unusual independence to take a much more active role in
managing their schools. "The Alum Rock Teachers
Association has been highly supportive," (Supt. William) Jefferds says, noting that the association urged
continuation of the minischool concept as part of their
contract negotiation packet. (McCarthy 1975, 7)

The end of the period of federal funding for this project was
now approaching, and there was no sign of another getting
underway.

9

1977-1981
Later Appraisals of Alum Rock

In 1977 the five-year Alum Rock project came to an end. Subsequent evaluations have tended to be less complimentary than those expressed during the trial period. Some of this later criticism was not directed against the project itself but rather against the limitations under which it was conducted. The crux of this argument was that these limitations prevented the project from being a "true" experiment for a voucher system. On this point there was general agreement. The question still remained, however, as to whether the project had any validity at all in the interest of the voucher debate. In this case, the reactions were much more diverse.

> The results . . . tell us only a limited amount that is useful in the way of formulating public policy because of the idiosyncratic nature of both the community in which the demonstration occurred and the demonstration itself. It was a hot house demonstration which has produced some marvelous anecdotes, but it does not permit drawing broad generalizations. (Doyle 1981, 74)

Considering the attention given during the first four years to the emergence and functioning of the minischools, it is surprising that during the fifth and final year they were discarded. Less surprising was the decision of Alum Rock authorities not to assume the additional costs the federal grant had been absorbing during the experiment (Salganik 1981,19). It seems that when federal funding came to an end, some opponents chose that as a chance to label the project a failure. This was unfair, if not dishonest. They understood the federal government had at the inception of planning for the project specified that funding would last for a period of from five to eight years. The end of federal support was not, therefore, a federal "withdrawal," but an end well known in advance.

It is true that the federal government did not attempt another project. One reason was a change in administrations. President Jimmy Carter, elected with the support of the National Education Association, pledged to create a U.S. Department of Education, as the NEA had urged. It was a pledge he kept.

It should not be surprising that he did not further promote a project established during the Richard Nixon years and continued during the Gerald Ford administration, a project that was anathema to the NEA leadership.

If, like many projected reforms, Alum Rock did not live up to the hopes of its supporters, neither did it justify the fears of its detractors. The public-school system was not destroyed—according to Laura Hersh Salganik, it was hardly dented.

One of the ironies relating to the argument for tuition vouchers is that though its current revival can be traced to the 1955 essay by Milton Friedman, "The Role of Government in Education," for most of its history it has been promoted by liberals—from Tom Paine, Thomas Jefferson, and John Stuart Mill to Christopher Jencks and Nat Hentoff. The fact that the Alum Rock experiment took place in the seventies during the Nixon years has caused it to become dubbed a conservative and suspect idea in the minds of many liberals, who might otherwise have been its natural supporters.

One who was concerned about this irony was New York Democratic Senator Daniel Patrick Moynihan. He remarked that, whereas in the late 1960s vouchers were regarded as a progressive proposal which could be supported by foundations and liberal faculty members, within a single decade they came to be regarded as a "bastion of white privilege and exclusivity."

Moynihan believed this would seriously reduce the likelihood of change which would, in turn,

> present immense problems for a person such as myself
> ... who was deeply involved in this issue long before
> it was either conservative or liberal. And if it prevails
> only as a conservative cause, it will have been a great
> failure of American liberalism not to have seen the
> essentially liberal nature of this pluralist proposition.
> (Moynihan 1981, 84)

After the interregnum of the Carter Administration, President Ronald Reagan picked up the cudgel to do battle for vouchers. This further tied the idea to conservatives and sent many liberals, at least at the national level, running for cover. Nevertheless, the "great failure" is now more a healthy reality than ever.

Moynihan also noted that the United States "is the only industrial democracy in the world that does not routinely provide aid to nonpublic schools as part of its educational system" (Moynihan 1981, 79). The senator from New York is one of the few Democrats at the national level who expresses such concern and openly indicates his support, just as he has for tax credits.

But one need not depend on judgments of Alum Rock, or conservatives, or liberals, for the general validity of vouchers. One need only look to Vermont and New Hampshire, states with a history of nonoperating public school districts and the use of public funds for tuition payments.

> In Vermont only two-thirds of the districts actually
> run schools. The other third have resident children but
> pay tuition for them to be educated in non-district
> schools, both public and private. There is in fact a
> continuous history of this tradition throughout New
> England. Vermont is the last surviving example of
> consequence, but it has existed in Massachusetts,
> Connecticut, and Maine. (Doyle 1981, 73)

Doyle concluded that, in Vermont, vouchers are noncontroversial, successful, workable, have been in place for well over a century and are neither racist nor elitist (Doyle 1981, 76).

It can be argued that Vermont is an anomaly, a small state that bears little resemblance to circumstances elsewhere. As a matter of fact 10,000 of today's more than 15,000 school districts in the nation are small, rural, or both, and a number of Vermont's school districts are more than adequate models for others to at least study, if not emulate.

It is also possible to look far beyond Vermont or U.S. borders for examples of a voucher system in operation. Funding of this type exists not only in Denmark, France, and England but also in Canada, the Netherlands, Australia, Belgium and Ireland, among others.

Australia is a particularly interesting example because, like the United States, it has a federal system with a written constitution, one key provision of which is almost identical to ours. It includes language prohibiting the establishment of religion, virtually identical to our First Amendment. Yet Australia funds private schools containing about thirty percent of the country's students. They have interpreted their constitutional provision precisely opposite from the way we have interpreted ours. Their view is that so long as all religions are treated equally, the state remains neutral.

> Section 116 of the Australian Constitution provides: "The Commonwealth shall not make any law for establishing any religion, or for imposing any religious observance, or for prohibiting the free exercise of any religion, and no religious test shall be required as a qualification for any office or public trust under the Commonwealth." (Doyle 1981, 72)

The Australian attitude seems reasonable—and not only to Australians. If all religions are treated equally, none being favored or opposed, where is the danger that the state is guilty of establishing any one of them? On the other hand, if the state supports nonsectarian agencies to the exclusion of religious ones, is it being neutral?

In Australia the coalition of support for education is broadly based, and interestingly enough, support for public education is higher than it would have been if there had not been general support for *both* public and private education (Doyle 1981, 78).

As a result of the ongoing debate in our own country over vouchers and tuition tax credits, more significant data is available than ever before concerning the quality of education in the nonpublic schools. In that category, the Catholic schools are particularly relevant to our inquiry because they represent more nonpublic schools than all other groups combined. In answer to the charge that Catholic schools are racially discriminatory, the facts indicate they are not.

In making a comparison of Catholic schools and public schools, Andrew Greeley's study shows that:

> thirty percent of Catholic schools have *few* blacks, compared to twenty-nine percent of the public schools;
>
> twenty-one percent of Catholic schools are half black, compared to twenty-eight percent of the public schools;
>
> twenty-two percent of the Catholic schools are mostly black, compared to twenty-four percent of the public schools; and
>
> seventeen percent of the Catholic schools are all black, compared to nineteen percent of the public schools.
>
> That is, thirty-nine percent of Catholic schools are mostly or all black, compared to forty-three percent of the public schools. (Greeley 1981, 12)

Not only are many of them composed largely or totally of blacks but most students at many Catholic schools are not even Catholic. What's more, a case could be made that Catholic schools in many areas have even made a greater contribution in Americanizing the children of immigrants than have the public schools. In fact, one of the reasons many of them were established in the nineteenth- and early twentieth-centuries was precisely to educate the new arrivals, such as the Irish and Italians, that the public schools were not prepared to handle and with whom much of the public wanted as little contact as possible. Memories of "No Irish need apply" remain in Irish Boston, and I recall a time when it was said that no Italian would ever be the principal of the high school at which I taught—something of a false prophecy, since in more recent times an Italian has become principal without repercussions. It is another of the ironies in American education that public-school advocates claim credit for much of the "Americanizing" that actually took place in the nonpublic schools, in the workplace, or in the general society.

One of the most outspoken supporters of vouchers is John E. Coons, whose long devotion to this endeavor has included trying with many collaborators to get it adopted by ballot initiative in California. (The bibliography includes a sample of Coons's work.) While developing legal viewpoints on the subject, as has Stephen Arons, and as anyone must do who is seriously interested in the topic, Coons has also written on the philosophical elements of the concept as well, perhaps as eloquently as anyone in the world. His concern with the child and the family, which any teacher should share, is evident.

> If too many of their pupils fall too far below those in comparable school districts on some standard meas-ure, the educators may be professionally embarrassed. However, in no case need they remember the names and faces of the victims. No teacher will be forced to share his home and his table with the failures who spent a thousand hours in his class before mercifully passing from his professional life and personal con-sciousness. Personal accountability of this sort is re-served for families . . . society and the school profes-sional blame the family for producing the education-ally defective product . . . One great virtue of family choice would be to resolve this irony by linking re-sponsibility to authority. (Coons and Sugarman 1978, 58)

He believes choice would benefit both the teacher, and schooling, since educators would no longer be able to dictate a program or procedure. It would be necessary to explain why particular approaches were being recommended, at least in instances where a student or parent wanted to know.

This would be similar to the relationship in other professions, of medical doctor to patient, or lawyer to client. It wouldn't end all problems or abuses, any more than it does in other fields, because the ordinary citizen is hesitant about challenging professionals with whom they deal, even in instances where great sums of money, or their lives, may be at stake. But it should provide educators with more autonomy and respect as the result of placing them in a more rewarding relationship with students and parents.

The nonpublic, or private, schools would seem to prove this assumption. Although, as a group, they have about half the resources of the public schools, and their teachers typically receive much lower salaries and fewer benefits, the nonpublic schools have much less turmoil. Teachers in private education are generally held in reasonably high esteem by their "customers." The element of choice, of each side being in the situation voluntarily, with the option of leaving it at anytime, means there is a higher degree of equality among all involved—teachers, administrators, students, and parents.

There is another voice that, for a unique reason, deserves attention.

> What would be the constitutional status of BEOG (Basic Education Opportunity Grant) legislation that provided tuition assistance only for students in *non-religious* elementary and secondary private schools? It would unquestionably be constitutional, would it not? In order to oppose the Moynihan BEOG proposal on constitutional grounds, then, one must believe that the First Amendment, which was adopted out of a special *solicitude* for religion, has the effect of not merely permitting but requiring a special *discrimination* against religion. Only students who wish to attend

religious schools not only *may* but absolutely *must* be excluded from a subsidy available to all others. That bizarre, antireligious result is simply too much to derive, it seems to me, from the mere prohibition of an establishment. (Scalia 1981, 184)

Five years after his published comments on BEOG, the then very young Antonin Scalia became a member of the United States Supreme Court. As Associate Justice, Scalia will likely have the opportunity to say more on this subject in the future and, if joined by at least four of his colleagues, that "saying" might one day reshape the educational system of the nation.

It is important to keep in mind that not all public school officials have been part of the anti-voucher contingent. When he was chancellor of the New York City Schools, Harvey Scribner (a former Vermonter), had been receptive:

Alternatives are what I'm after, choices that parents and students can make for themselves. I'd like to see the voucher concept—parents being able to choose the kind of education they want for their children—become part of the public school system. (Nat Hentoff 1977, 196)

In 1977 the U.S. Supreme Court added items to the list of the forms of assistance that nonpublic schools might receive. Diagnostic services provided on nonpublic school premises, and therapeutic, guidance, and remedial services provided by public employees on sites not identified with nonpublic schools were deemed constitutional (*Wolman v. Walter*).

In that same year, in Missouri, a group of taxpayers made the charge in court that the "secular humanism" taught in the public schools is a religion. E. G. West reported in "The Perils of Public Education":

The only fair way to support education according to the Missouri plaintiffs is the introduction of the voucher system. (West 1977, 688)

As to the need for the wisdom and order of governmental laws and regulations to assure effective education and good citizenship, Coons argued that regulations concerning content and method were rarely adopted with the interest of the children as the principal object. It was more likely they resulted from the requests, or pressure, of some activist group. In these circumstances, legislators find it easier to satisfy the group by enacting their requests than to turn them down. Requirements for teaching about patriotism, kindness to animals, and the like, tend to anger no one but they also seldom have any serious impact on the behavior of schools or teachers, and have even less connection to any benefit to pupils (Coons and Sugarman 1978, 39).

Coons noted that in other examples of government-provided services, such as charity hospitals, public housing, and food programs, it is unthinkable that government would mandate in such detail as it does to the schools. The government doesn't tell the family how often they should go to the hospital, and on what schedule; it doesn't require that food can be obtained only if the government establishes the menu and operates the kitchen; yet it has no hesitancy in directing a child about what school to attend, on what days, in what classes, with which teachers, and what books to read.

The other programs, which already have so much choice, are being given even more under programs involving food stamps and Medicaid. Even in housing programs vouchers are being considered in place of the projects which have proven to be ineffective, if not disastrous (Coons and Sugarman 1978, 66-67).

Coons also makes the point that civil libertarians defend variety in the arts, and public funding of a variety of personal expressions in this field, yet at the same time they argue for uniformity in education—an irony of which they seem blissfully unaware (Coons and Sugarman 1978, 104).

One of the most common arguments in support of choice is that those who educate their children privately, whether in a nonpublic school, with tutors, or at home, must pay twice for that option since they still must pay to support the public schools as well. Whatever the theoretical merits of that argument may be and no matter how strongly they may be defended, so far they have had little effect on resolving the issue.

In Colorado, Representative Thomas G. Tancredo, chairman of the House Education Committee, began the 1980s with an effort to have a voucher system for support of higher education in that state adopted through a statewide referendum. While student choice would be the base for any such campaign, he said the main reason for his support was that it would reduce the legislature's involvement in the management of colleges and universities, an argument educators should cheer. Rep. Tancredo reported having a list of about one hundred supporters, mostly from public colleges and universities in the Denver area.

In Colorado's other chamber, Senator Hugh C. Fowler said vouchers would make students aware of the size of the state's subsidy of higher education and might encourage public support for increased expenditures.

In Kansas, the senate education committee recommended a legislative study of a voucher proposal to provide $35 per credit-hour for Kansas residents who were attending any of the sixty public and private postsecondary institutions within the state (Jacobson 1980, 4).

In California, John Coons strengthened his argument about the benefits vouchers would extend to teachers. Besides believing that it would at last make professionals of public school teachers, he also believed that it could make them prosperous ones as well. He based that on the belief that schools would be smaller and would place a much heavier emphasis on the role of teachers, rather than on other subsidiary or peripheral personnel. If a ten teacher school in 1981 had two hundred pupils receiving a voucher or scholarship for $2,300 each, it is likely their salaries would be appreciably higher than they were in the public schools of that time (Coons 1981, 99).

By 1990 the per pupil costs in the nation's public schools approached $5,000, so a class of thirty pupils cost the taxpayer nearly $150,000 while the average classroom teacher was paid about $30,000 for the school year. The percentage of public school costs caused by teacher salaries has been declining for years. Clearly, a different arrangement could result in increased salaries, which many believe would attract more and better qualified individuals into the profession and at no increase in overall costs.

Denis Doyle provided further argument countering some of the charges against nonpublic education. While there is often the implication, if not the outright statement, that nonpublic schools are elitist and racist, the charge is not supported by the evidence—those making the charge rarely cite a specific instance, of which there are more than a few in the public school sector.

> In a recent publication by the Bureau of the Census, for example, Susanne Bianchi concludes that, controlling for socio-economic factors, the fact of being white increases the probability of private school attendance by only one percent. This is probably the strongest evidence we have to date suggesting that race or ethnicity is not the key variable in private school attendance. (Doyle 1981, 74)

Frederick Weintraub added to the list of precedents, noting that local and state governments have historically been heavily involved in both the financing and placement of handicapped children in private schools, as has the federal government. Parents of such children have been able to deduct such costs from their federal income tax forms, the theory being that this expense was being incurred for medical reasons rather than educational ones. Even accepting this rationale, it is difficult to understand why a medical cost incurred in a private institution, especially when there are public ones available, is deductible while an educational cost under the same circumstances is not.

In 1965 when the Elementary and Secondary Education Act became law, the federal role in education was significantly expanded. Part B of Title I of that act provides aid to state-supported schools and institutions, a program primarily designed to assist children who are in state institutions for the retarded or state schools for the deaf and blind. However, a private school receiving state aid was treated as a state-supported institution. States gave federal project grants to private schools and do so to this day (Weintraub 1981, 51).

As a consequence, many private schools for the handicapped receive eighty, ninety, or even one-hundred percent of their funds from public sources. If such a school, totally funded by government money, is a private school, how can other private schools be denied support? Is it legal, constitutional, or even fair to discriminate in such a manner against conventional students? Can a student be denied public funding for a school of his or her choice today because of a lack of a handicap and receive it next week if they should have a crippling accident or illness? And how "private" is a private school that is fully funded by the government? (Weintraub 1981, 52).

That question, and the accompanying determination of what a public school is, has yet to be answered.

10

1982-1985
Crisis and Gradual Change

Many advocates of vouchers began to drop from the field and others gave evidence of becoming a bit discouraged. For example, when John Coons was asked in an interview what he saw in the future for the reform of school finance, he replied:

> Not much. All the signs are that the systems are comfortably ossified. They are well designed to serve their managers and those who can afford to choose their residences. There is not much in it for the legislator who would like to change it . . . In California, some of us will continue to try to reverse this trend through the initiative process, but I have to concede that the unions and the managers are a formidable force in favor of the status quo. (*Phi Delta Kappan*, March 1983, 480)

Considering the fact that although more than two centuries have passed since the idea was first suggested and it still has not been implemented to any significant degree in elementary and basic education, a bit of pessimism is perhaps justified.

It is possible, however, that the legal battle for general aid to all students, including those in nonpublic schools, may be

won and is over, thanks to Minnesota. From this state has come
the court case that may have decided the issue.

As early as 1955, Minnesota permitted state tax deductions
for school expenses, and in the mid-1980s it was estimated that
as many as sixty percent of the people used the deduction to
send their children to public schools. Deductions are permitted
for up to $650 for each elementary student and $1,000 for each
high school student (Nathan 1985, 478).

This issue finally came before the U.S. Supreme Court
in the case of *Mueller v. Allen* in 1983. A 5-4 division upheld a
Minnesota law allowing the deduction on state income taxes
for tuition, textbooks, and transportation expenses incurred in
the education of students in either public or nonpublic elementary and secondary schools.

The Court majority consisted of Associate (now Chief)
Justice William H. Rehnquist, who wrote the opinion, Chief
Justice Warren Burger, and Associate Justices Byron White,
Lewis Powell, Jr., and Sandra Day O'Connor. Dissenting were
Associate Justices Marshall, Brennan, Blackmun, and Stevens.

In the Court's view:

A State's decision to defray the cost of educational
expenses incurred by parents—regardless of the type
of schools their children attend—evidences a purpose
that is both secular and understandable. An educated
populace is essential to the political and economic
health of any community, and a State's efforts to assist
parents in meeting the rising costs of educational
expenses plainly serves this secular purpose of ensuring that the State's citizenry is well educated. Similarly, Minnesota, like other States, could conclude that
there is a strong public interest in assuring the continued financial health of private schools, both sectarian
and nonsectarian. By educating a substantial number
of students such schools relieve public schools of a
correspondingly great burden—to the benefit of all
taxpayers. In addition, private schools may serve as a
benchmark for public schools in a manner analogous

to the "TVA yardstick" for private power companies.
(*Mueller v. Allen* 1983, 395)

And:

Most importantly, the deduction is available for educational expenses incurred by all parents, including
those whose children attend nonsectarian private
schools or sectarian private schools.(*Mueller v. Allen*
1983, 397)

The decision's narrowness partially obscured the Court's
continuing consistency in support of educational assistance
available to all students. The decision validated forms of such
aid existing in sections of the New England states, in Washington, and in Milwaukee, Wisconsin.

In more than 30 Maine towns that lack high schools of
their own, for example, students have been allowed to
attend any one of several public, private, or parochial
high schools, with the towns paying their tuition. "We
never called them voucher plans, but they serve the
same purpose," noted Richard Redmond, deputy com-
missioner of education in Maine. (Nathan 1985, 478)

In 1985, Minnesota began allowing public school juniors
and seniors to attend state colleges, other postsecondary
schools, or Minnesota private liberal arts colleges, for high
school and college credit at public expense.

In Milwaukee, Wisconsin, students can attend a traditional
neighborhood school or enroll in one of forty career and other
specialty programs located throughout the city.

In the state of Washington, teenagers who have not
succeeded in the public schools are provided with the means to
attend *educational clinics,* including those operated by for-profit
groups as well as by private, nonprofit groups and antipoverty
agencies. Former public-school teachers staff some of the
clinics, which implies that they didn't leave their former

positions because of unhappiness with either the students or education.

In the Midwest:

> Native American parents tried unsuccessfully to convince the local public school to change curriculum materials and instructional approaches to increase the success rate of their children. Met with hostile reactions, the Ojibways, with the aid of federal funds, established their own schools, "which significantly improved their children's achievement." (Cromley 1985)

The concept has continued to advance in areas beyond the U.S., and in the course of development it has provided additional proof that teachers will, indeed, react favorably under this new "choice" environment and will take the initiative whenever circumstances permit them to do so. In Canada,

> denominational school funding developed with the British North America Act (BNAA) in 1867; in the Netherlands, full financial equality between public and private education was achieved in 1917. In contrast, large-scale public support of nonpublic institutions in England. . . . began in 1945. The Canadian provinces of Quebec and British Columbia initiated provincial grants to independent schools in 1968 and 1977 respectively. And farther from the United States, Australia enacted major funding programs for both denominational and independent schools in the 1970s. (Sherman 1983, 72)

In 1985 Peter Brimelow commented on conditions in British Columbia:

> Canadian economist Stephen T. Easton, of British Columbia's Simon Fraser University, reports that channeling government education subsidies directly to private schools in that province has resulted in an

unexpected blossoming of teachers declaring independence to start their own schools. (Brimelow 1985, 353)

Brimelow added his opinion that public education is "a curious and anomalous" socialistic enterprise, whose chronic problems will remain until it has to deal with competition.

As the Alum Rock project receded into the past, it continued to draw attention and new evaluations. In 1984, almost a decade after its conclusion, David K. Cohen and Eleanor Farrar analyzed it with less enthusiasm than had Joel Levin after the first and second years of operation, but with a more positive conclusion than Laura Hersh Salganik had reached in 1981.

From the perspective of promoting diversity . . . The voucher demonstration in Alum Rock increased professionals' ability to choose and design their work settings, and made it possible for parents to select among alternatives. If choice and diversity are good, then schools in Alum Rock were better places. (Cohen and Farrar 1984, 265-66)

Nathan Glazer contributed an unusual insight into the effect of nonpublic schools upon discrimination practices within their geographic areas.

When one's child attends private school, one is not required to move to get into the school of one's choice, and residential mobility for educational reasons is reduced. (Glazer 1983, 95)

Remember, the nonpublic schools are not as segregated—racially, economically, or even religiously—as is often claimed. Inner-city schools tend to be integrated, whether public or private, but, according to Glazer, where the private schools are present, "white flight" tends to be absent.

On the other side of the coin, however, Richard J. Murnane, points out a possible weakness in the funding of education with tuition tax credits and, by implication, vouchers.

> Recent U.S. experiences with third-party payment systems in the health and nursing home industries indicate that the potential for fraud is very great. (Murnane 1983, 220)

This is certainly a possibility. It is countered by experience with the GI Bill, and other third-party funding approaches, both in basic and higher education. Fraud or abuse has occurred but on a relatively minor scale. It should also be remembered that fraud and abuse exist in the present system, with little option for correction by individual parents or students.

There is also a significant difference between most other third-party payments and those in education. Medicare, Medicaid, food stamps, and the like are relatively open-ended programs, either in terms of what is available in a given year, or the number of years one may be covered; in some instances both of these conditions apply. Education assistance, on the other hand, tends to be for limited amounts of both money and time. Any veteran who permitted fraudulent use of this benefit—for example, allowing a fly-by-night or "paper" school to claim tuition reimbursement for his or her non-attendance—would thereby lose later use of the benefit for educational advancement, as well as running the risk of criminal penalties.

Another development of the early eighties was the conclusion of a massive study of the public schools. Conducted by John I. Goodlad, the results were published in 1984 as *A Place Called School*. The tone is temperate, the documentation and extent of the study is impressive, and the findings are largely consistent with those that appeared earlier.

> I do in fact doubt that schooling, as presently conceived and conducted, is capable of providing large segments of young people with the education they and this democracy require, and I include among these young people a significant proportion of those now "making it." (Goodlad 1984, 91)

The latter point is important. Many public school critics have noted its obvious failures, and its inability to assist the disadvantaged, the poor, the unusual, student—including many who are bright, creative, and well-adjusted. Goodlad concluded it isn't working for many who emerge successfully from its embrace. Teachers will recognize the truth of that comment. Many students succeed despite, not because of, schooling.

Unfortunately, as indicated in an earlier chapter, educators tend not to be readers of professional material, and probably only a very limited number of the nation's teachers have read his report, or those of others, and a goodly number may have never even heard of it. Still, changes do seem to be underway. Bit by bit, state by state, the system is opening up. While the pace may not seem swift enough to meet the need, and there is no certainty as to the final outcome, it is perhaps both desirable and inevitable that it take place in this manner.

Revolution by evolution permits continual adjustments along the way, and the opportunity to benefit from the experiences of the early pioneers. Besides, there is no way for the institution of public schooling in the United States, being as large as it is, to be transformed overnight, not even if it were— as it is in most other western democracies—a national system. A massive structure involving fifty states, more than fifteen thousand school districts, millions of teachers, tens of millions of students, and hundreds of billions of capital investment and annual expenditures, has an institutional inertia that does not permit rapid alterations. This is not to say it cannot be altered, but only that it requires great patience, persistence, and persuasion to bring it about. As a matter of fact, public perceptions and opinion do seem to be changing, for there is today a growing awareness that

> (T)he nineteenth century common school provided anything but a uniform and common education . . . Within the common school there were different schooling experiences for various racial, ethnic, social, and religious groups. Differences in the availability of private schools, residential location, political power, race, and income were reflected to a great extent in schools that were heavily stratified. (Henry Levin 1982, 16)

Some people are concerned that private choices may not lead to the proper social results. This argument against family choice lacks convincing evidence. Over the generations tens of millions of students have attended nonpublic schools. There is no evidence that they have been in any way inferior to citizens produced by the public-school system. James S. Coleman has suggested that, if anything, the truth is that the nonpublic schools, specifically the Catholic parochial schools, have done a better job in this regard than the public institutions. And they have done it not only for Catholics but for non-Catholics as well, and not only for whites but for nonwhites. (Coleman and Hoffer 1987, 5)

It should also be remembered that the Founding Fathers, who established this nation and wrote the United States Constitution, were themselves products either of religiously affiliated private schools, or of a tutoring program, or of home schooling. A few were self-taught. This did not prevent them from achieving desirable social results or from establishing "social cohesion"—to counter another rhetorical complaint about the possible dangers of vouchers.

In the view of Henry M. Levin, the challenge of vouchers and tuition tax credits may at least motivate the public-school system to increase the options for students and parents, even if vouchers and credits do not become realities. If support for them did not exist there would probably not be the current movement toward alternative schools, open enrollments, and other reforms in the public school arena (Levin 1982, 44).

During this time Stephen Arons's work on the First Amendment's implications for separation of school and state culminated in the publication of *Compelling Belief*, which to some represented a compelling argument. Arons makes the point that for a citizen to pay a state tax in support of government schools in addition to making private payments in the exercise of the First Amendment right to choose a school is no more constitutionally acceptable than it is for a citizen to be forced to pay a poll tax in order to exercise the right to vote (Arons 1983, 211).

In one of his articles, "The Separation of School and State: *Pierce* Reconsidered," he makes an important point:

If the First Amendment is applied to the reality of schooling as it has developed in this century, the conclusion must be that individual liberty, the healthy functioning of the political system, and the preservation of a truly public and governable public-school system require a separation of school and state. (Arons 1976, 212-13)

From Minnesota came the voice of Joe Nathan, a public school teacher and administrator:

We have never provided equal opportunity in education. If we stick to our present system of public and private schools, we will fall farther and farther short of our ideals. . . . For more than 200 years, there has been tension between providing equal opportunity and limiting individual freedom . . . The voucher concept offers an opportunity to join these conflicting ideas. (Nathan, 1983, 147)

Thomas James added further evidence that government schools had not been the great leveler in the past as their advocates maintain:

One study has shown that by 1879 the academies, along with the preparatory departments that played a similar role as extensions of private colleges, enrolled about 73 percent of all students at the secondary level in the United States. As the public high school took hold, the number fell to 32 percent a mere ten years later. (James 1983, 61)

Nathan Glazer agreed:

I am convinced that the conflicts of values in this country today . . . . are so great that the vision of a truly common school, in which all are educated together, simply will not work. Fortunately, for its hopes for success, the common school, whatever its ideology, has not, for most of its history, been like that, nor are most public schools like that today. (Glazer 1983, 100)

As for precedents for government aid to nongovernment schools, Dennis Encarnation gave this assessment:

When aid from both direct and indirect government sources was added together using available data, it made up an estimated one-quarter of total nonpublic-school resources from all public and private sources during the 1970-71 school year. Given expanded aid programs . . . it is very unlikely that the relative importance of government financial support has diminished with time. (Encarnation 1983, 193)

It should be recalled that the ongoing "crisis" in education, is not really that; it is a crisis in public schooling. Education is always subject to criticism but the constant barrage since at least 1953, when Arthur Bestor's *Educational Wastelands* was published, has been primarily in and about the public schools.

Like all American institutions, nonpublic schools could use more money, but the various problems of "education" with which we are all familiar are more properly regarded as a problem of public "schooling." Numerous surveys and studies have shown that satisfaction in nonpublic schools, on the part of students, parents, teachers (despite their lower pay) and everyone else is much higher than in the public schools. Strikes are virtually unknown. Yet the nonpublic schools, as a group, have less of almost everything and what they have is of a poorer quality—older buildings, textbooks, etc.—in comparison to the public schools. The reason for the satisfaction seems to stem from the condition of choice.

The variety that exists in nonpublic schools also precludes what William von Humboldt regarded as the major problems of government-controlled education: uniform treatment of individuals and mediocrity. Like Adam Smith, Humboldt reasoned that

the profit motive would encourage better teaching, which would in time result in a greater demand for

education. He noticed that teachers educate themselves better when their fortunes depend on their own
efforts, than when their chances of promotion rest on
what they are led to expect from the state. (O'Donnell
1985, 78)

Frank Newman suggested that

a new program should be created, based on the basic
elements of the GI Bill, providing student aid in return
for community service on the part of young men and
women. (Newman 1985, xix)

AFT President Albert Shanker, commenting on research
showing that the average education student has an SAT score
40 points below the national average noted that superintendents complicate this by hiring the worst of the new teachers
because they give less trouble.

I have personally seen one teacher knowingly hired with
false credentials—the college transcripts presented belonged
to someone with the same name. I know of another person who
was selected for department chairman after the administration
had been specifically advised that, of all the teachers interested
in the position, this was the one who was least qualified on the
basis of leadership ability, creative imagination and originality,
a person who lacked the ability to be independent enough to
differ with the central administration if the need arose. Perhaps
the superintendent selected that person for those very weak-
nesses.

Other educators can undoubtedly supply their own examples. It does indeed happen, and the reason Shanker gave
for the superintendent's attraction to mediocrity is probably accurate. Shanker has also warned that "If we don't improve the
public schools, people will turn to private schools." To which
Peter Brimelow responded:

Aha! Doesn't this concede the argument that stronger
private schools will keep the public sector honest?
Changing fronts adroitly, Shanker instantly draws an
ingenious distinction between the idea of competition,

which he describes as stimulative, and the reality, which he argues would be destructive. But his debating skill does not quite cover the hole in his argument. (Brimelow 1985, 353)

Lawrence Uzzell identifies two groups of serious reformers: the "neocentralists," who would further centralize government schools with full state funding or, as in Hawaii, with a statewide school district; and the "neopluralists," who would decentralize or localize schools.

The neopluralists believe that most of what we now call "education policy" should be made by people in daily contact with real children . . . . Their spokesmen include Stephen Arons, author of a brilliant theoretical critique of monopoly schooling, and Joe Nathan, godfather of the controversial Minnesota voucher proposal that was upheld early in 1983 by the Supreme Court. (Uzzell 1985,14)

By the mid-eighties only forty cents of each government school dollar was going to the classroom teacher, a circumstance that could be expected to change in voucher schools managed by the faculty.

Parents would be likely to support a redistribution favoring teachers for the same reason that so many of them now pay tuition in private schools; that is, they seek good teaching and small classes, not more administration. (Coons 1985, 11)

Public officials began openly supporting vouchers, although not necessarily in exact agreement about the same form. Supporters included Tenn. Governor Lamar Alexander and Florida Sen. Jack Gordon.

In the 1983 Gallup Poll of the Public's Attitudes toward the Public Schools, fifty-one percent of the public favored a voucher plan as did sixty-four percent of blacks and sixty percent of those between 18 and 29.

In 1985 William Coats, the Executive Director of the Education Voucher Institute of Farmington, Michigan, thought the public school establishment would never support any voucher proposal. Perhaps not, but public opinion polls reveal that a significant percentage of public school teachers support the voucher concept. They need to be recognized and organized for their input is invaluable.

The Institute has since ceased to exist and Coats is part of the establishment about which he worried. In 1987, after he had become the Superintendent in the Anchorage, Alaska School District, he wrote the author to say he continues "to believe that free market concepts such as parental choice and competition not only have a place in public education but must operate to some degree in order for public schools to survive."

A superintendent who believes differently is Lew Finch, who has said it is "a cruel hoax" to suggest that vouchers would give all students access to excellent programs (Finch 1985, 12). First, no one has suggested that a voucher program would assure all students having access to excellent programs. Repeatedly, proponents have cautioned that no system is perfect. Second, do "all students" have such access now? Finch, whose special interest shows, implies they do. The "cruel hoax" is the one perpetrated by public schools that pretend to do what they do not, and probably cannot, do.

Another straw man that Finch puts forward in his opposition is the view that there is an

> absence of documented experience and research to suggest that a voucher plan is likely to improve learning for the majority of students. A substantial body of knowledge exists showing what will improve learning, but an open voucher system is not identified as a factor contributing to effective schools. (Finch 1985, 11)

Too many public-school people like Finch create a Catch 22 situation by opposing voucher projects and then, as here, citing the lack of research data as an argument against vouchers. Furthermore, as has been indicated, a wide variety of voucher programs do exist in the nation: for typical students in places like Vermont, New Hampshire, and Maine, for special education students in many places and, of course, for veterans under the GI Bill. The GI Bill, used by over 17,000,000 veterans, in addition to other federal and state programs providing student grants, more than prove "that a voucher plan is likely to improve learning for the majority of students."

In 1985 the Reagan Administration again proposed, as it had in 1983, converting the Title I program to vouchers, averaging about $600 per pupil. Education Secretary William J. Bennett argued that a $600 voucher could make a considerable difference for many youngsters, especially when one considers that the average tuition in private elementary schools was only $635.

Bennett also noted that public opinion polls show low-income and minority parents are among the strongest supporters of vouchers. As for the argument that public schools will not be able to compete with private schools, he said that seventy-nine percent of those who have the funds to choose any school in the nation choose a public school. This is slightly below the eighty-two percent that attend public schools in France where they have had vouchers since the early 1950s.

Sen. Orrin G. Hatch (R.-Utah) guaranteed this approach would have high priority in the United States Senate, but that didn't happen and the bill died with the session at the end of 1986.

A middle ground is struck by Mario D. Fantini, Dean of the School of Education at the University of Massachusetts, who has long worked for options within the public school framework. He argues that the main difference between private and public education is the right of choice and that the public schools try to make everyone fit the system even though there is no best way either to teach or to learn. Promoting choice within public schools, therefore, is a win-win proposition for everyone. If the public schools do not begin to present meaningful choices, however, then "a voucher system is in the cards for the future."

Patrick Cox, an analyst for the American Studies Institute in Phoenix, Arizona, argues that teachers should work for parents, not politicians. He would also change our terminology and call public schools government schools and refer to private schools as voluntary schools. He regards "public" and "private" references to schools as terms taught us by the government. *USA Today*, reporting this story, added some thoughts from a random selection of Americans across the country, who were asked how they felt about school vouchers. Most of those reported in the story supported them. They included Lloyd Graf, 62, a shipping clerk from Loma Linda, California; Michael McDonald, 28, a Green Bay, Wisconsin accountant; Julianna Williams, a 29-year-old word processor from Houston, Texas, who believes they would be especially helpful for underprivileged children; and Ed Watkins, a 41-year-old construction estimator from Alexandria, Virginia, who regards vouchers as "a step in the right direction" and favors testing the idea (*USA Today*, Dec. 11, 1985, 10A).

Another supporter was Diane Ravitch, who has written extensively about education. Noting the general use of student grants for low-income students to attend either public or private institutions of higher education, she added, "it is difficult to see why this approach is appropriate for college, but not for schooling" (Ravitch 1985, 168).

Peter Brimelow regards public schooling as "the American version of Soviet agriculture, beyond help as currently organized because its incentive structure is all wrong" and says this socialized monopoly can be cured by competition such as vouchers would provide (Brimelow 1985, 351, 352).

In 1985 support definitely seemed to be growing.

11

1986-89
Variations on the Theme

In 1986 there was activity in support of family choice; at the same time evidence was accumulating that a change in the schooling system is necessary. A report by the National Coalition of Advocates for Students (NCAS) claimed that the school policies of tracking and sorting students were having "a resegregating effect" which is perceived as a disadvantage to blacks and Hispanics, and is a cause of higher dropout rates in the population of nonwhite students. The report said blacks drop out at twice the rate of whites and the rate reaches eighty percent for Puerto Rican students and eighty-five percent for Native Americans in some schools (McGuire 1986, 15). Surely, no form of a voucher system, or any other "choice" option, could produce worse results.

Public school teachers are aware of their system's shortcomings, especially in urban centers. Whatever their organizational leaders may maintain, however they may argue on behalf of public schools against the "threat" of nonpublic schools, teachers know better. The proof is that public school teachers send their own children to nonpublic schools in greater proportion than do other parents.

The American Enterprise Institute reports that in Chicago, for example, forty-six percent of that system's teachers send their children to private schools, compared to twenty-three percent of the parents who are not public school teachers. In Albuquerque, the comparative percentages are 30 and 14; in Austin, Texas, twenty-five and thirteen; and so on in similar ratios around the nation (*The Wall Street Journal*, August 28, 1986, 14). Public school teachers prefer private schools for their own children. Do they know something their leaders don't? Do they think private schools are inferior, or racist, or destructive of the general consensus and the need for "social cohesion"? Do they oppose personal choice? Would they object to a tuition voucher assisting their educational independence?

The annual Gallup Poll of the Public's Attitudes toward the Public Schools, reported annually in *Phi Delta Kappan*, for the sixth time in sixteen years (1970, 1971, 1981, 1983, 1985, and 1986), for the second year in a row, and for the third time in four years, asked this question:

> In some nations the government allots a certain amount of money for each child for his education. The parents can send the child to any public, parochial or private school they choose. This is called the "voucher system." Would you like to see such an idea adopted in this country?

In 1986 forty-six percent said yes, forty-one percent said no, and thirteen percent had no opinion. Those with no children in school voted 44-41-15; public school parents favored the idea 51-41-8; and the nonpublic school parents tally was 64-28-8. In other words, those directly affected by the decision favored it by clear majorities, while those without children in school were narrowly divided on the question. For the same six Gallup Polls, the overall totals were:

Year	Yes	No	No opinion
1970	43	46	11
1971	38	44	18
1981	43	41	16
1983	51	38	11
1985	45	40	15
1986	46	41	13

Thus, for sixteen years, a near-majority plurality, or an actual majority, has favored the system and, since 1981, those in favor have always outnumbered those opposed.

The 1986 survey showed:

Nonwhites favor adoption of the system by a wide margin (54 percent to 33 percent). Similarly, those under thirty, Catholics, persons residing in inner cities, and those who are dissatisfied with the performance of the public schools (i.e., give them a D or Failing grade) support the adoption of the voucher system by about a 5-3 margin. (Alec M. Gallup 1986, 58)

Among voucher advocates, perhaps the under-thirty subgroup is the most encouraging support. If they don't change their minds, they could provide a majority in a few years, perhaps a politically effective majority.

A variation of this periodic question in the Gallup Polls came in early 1988 when the organization was polling for the Times Mirror Company. This nationwide survey asked citizens whether they were more or less "likely to vote for a candidate who supports giving parents vouchers to pay for their kids' education." Omitting those who didn't express a preference, the results were that forty-nine percent were more likely to vote for such a candidate and only twenty-seven percent were less likely.

The poll, part of a series, also divided the public into nine subcategories—four of which were oriented toward the Republicans and five toward the Democrats. Of these nine groups only one, a Democratic group representing seven percent of all voters, was less likely to support such a candidate and by a thirty-three to forty-one percent ratio (*Newsweek*, May 16, 1988, p. 8). It seems that the ongoing debate in favor of vouchers is gradually making an impression, even if it is not making headline news.

Efficiencies that could result from family choice and professional autonomy for teachers might solve the unending fiscal crisis of public schooling. Surveys of parents showed most of them are concerned about teacher quality and favor small schools, especially neighborhood schools. Teachers, on the other hand, tend to be more concerned with class size. The concern of the parents has been backed up by research that proves small schools are more important to students than small classes. When students complain of being a number, it is usually because of the size of the institution they are attending.

In Japan, whose students' math scores consistently out-rank those in the United States and other nations, the typical math class may have seventy-one students. This is not an argument for classes of that size in this country but it certainly is proof that students in such classes can be achievers.

At the same time, the percentage of the public school budget devoted to teachers has been declining for years. Where not too many years ago it was fifty-six percent, or more, it now is in the thirty-seven to forty percent range. The remainder goes to larger administrative staffs than schools need, or parents desire; to large schools which increase, not decrease, costs; to transportation costs (most of which, contrary to public opinion, are not caused by busing for desegregation but by the creation of large central schools); to fund ineffective but expensive mandates that elected officials cannot seem to refrain from adopting; and to numerous other programs which, while they may be supported by a number of citizens, would not likely be implemented in schools created by teachers and selected by students and their parents.

On the other hand, the nonpublic school budgets reveal that their per-pupil costs average much less than public schools and without a decline in academic achievement.

Consider the following statement about the variance in expenses incurred by municipal government:

> A recent study of 121 cities by the National Center for Policy Analysis (NCPA) concluded that some cities pay seven times more than others for janitorial services, six times more for street cleaning, 11 times more per ton for trash collection, four times more per ton for asphalt paving, and more than three times more for maintenance of traffic signals. (Lieberman, June 1986, 732)

Other studies have indicated that a similar variance in costs exists for education. Comparable schools, in both higher and basic education, have differences in per-pupil costs of two-to-one or more. If schools were competing with one another, the style of the efficient ones might be more generally adopted.

While the purpose of this volume is to present a history of the voucher idea rather than possible alternate school models, it is certainly conceivable that an effective school could be created with higher average teacher salaries and lower average per-pupil costs than the present system. Much could be implemented within the present system. The supportive research is there, but it is ignored, sometimes intentionally so, because it indicates changes in structure, processes, and roles unwelcome to many now in control. In this case, the problem is not lack of money; it is lack of will.

Another 1986 development was the explosion of a delayed time bomb, set ticking by the U.S. Supreme Court's 1975 *Wood v. Strickland* decision. It held that public school officials could be liable for damages if students were not properly treated. Late in 1986 U.S. District Judge Thomas G. Hull in Greeneville, Tennessee awarded more than $50,000 to seven fundamentalist Christian families who paid to send their children to private schools so they would not have to read public-school textbbooks they found religiously offensive.

The judge said "the school board violated the families' civil rights by forcing their children to remain in reading classes when their parents believed their religious beliefs were being undermined by material in the 1983 edition of the Holt, Rinehart, Winston reading series." Hull said, "the children should be allowed to 'opt out' of religiously offensive reading classes" (*The Patriot*, Dec. 16, 1986, A1).

The parents in this case, among other things, objected to the use of *The Wizard of Oz* in a classroom attended by their child because of its reference to a "wicked witch." That has been a cause of amusement in some quarters, even if the court ruling has not. Admittedly, the presence of *The Wizard of Oz* in the curriculum, or its absence, is not likely to save the world. With the story televised at least once a year, not many Americans can remain forever unaware of it. Still, what is so terrible about family choice that permits a parent to send a child to a school with or without *The Wizard*, as they wish?

The decision was appealed and overturned but Judge Hull's ruling reverberated throughout the public education community. Appalled by the decision, and by the dollars awarded, public educators proclaim the impossibility of operating a school that can please everybody.

Absolutely. They have it right.

They seem, however, unable to arrive at the logical conclusion: If it is impossible, then why try to operate schools for everybody? Why not have everybody choose their own school? Why not place the individual before the institution? Institutions, after all, are but means to ends, not ends in themselves.

The nation has not heard the last of this type of controversy. As long as parents and students are coerced by the state, some will fight back.

Other developments include the introduction of a program in Minnesota whereby the state will pay toward the costs of college students who would normally be in the 11th or 12th grade, where the state would be paying for their education anyway, through its support of the public schools.

As the program continues, students electing this option seem to do as well in college as those who normally attend after high school graduation, although there have been complaints from some in the public schools who bemoan the loss of funds they would otherwise receive. They seem to feel students should be kept hostage a few years longer as a source of income.

Representative John Brandl, also a public affairs professor at the Hubert Humphrey Institute and the author of an educational voucher bill, argued that Minnesota's educational problems are too serious for piecemeal approaches. The system, he argued, requires more than "mere tinkering," and additional money to the K-12 system should only be provided if corresponding change is initiated. As a result the Minnesota Education Association withdrew its endorsement of his reelection bid. He won anyway (Mazzoni and Sullivan 1986, 189 and 192).

The changes in Minnesota were strongly urged by a report in 1982 by the Citizens League, an independent public interest organization which called for deregulation, decentralization, and parent choice in education. Support also came from Public School Incentives, a nonprofit corporation formed to "create alternatives in public school education," from the Minnesota Business Partnership, and from Governor Rudy Perpich (Mazzoni and Sullivan 1986, 189-190).

> The most far-reaching of the governor's recommendations is granting every Minnesota student by 1988-89 the right to attend any of the state's public schools, regardless of district boundaries. State school funding—and in the Perpich plan the state would pay the costs for all basic foundation aid—would follow the student. (Mazzoni and Sullivan 1986,192-93)

Those who thought this couldn't possibly occur were undoubtedly surprised when it was passed by the legislature in early 1988, to be phased in over the next few school years. This success, it was argued, came about because of the gradualist approach that concerned Representative Brandl.

In 1985, as mentioned, high school juniors and seniors were allowed to attend colleges and universities with state support. In 1987, "at risk" students could transfer to another district, followed by state funding. In 1987-88, fourteen hundred of them did just that, including the return of seven hundred who had dropped out earlier. Also in 1987, a voluntary interdistrict enrollment plan was begun, with 153 districts scheduled to participate in 1988-89. In 1988 adults were allowed to return to high school to earn a diploma if they had at least finished tenth grade and were receiving public assistance.

These steps, each of which was successful, or promised to be so, helped obtain the passage of the statewide open-enrollment plan in the spring of 1988. The plan took effect in 1989-90 for the state's 435 school districts, each of which has more than one thousand students. Those districts with a smaller student body have until 1990-91 before they have to take part. Each district must develop a plan for the admission of transfer students. They do have the option of accepting none at all, but if they once accept a student, they must accept everyone applying, provided there is space (William Snider, *Education Week*, May 4, 1988, pp. 1, 13).

Minnesota has the highest graduation rate in the nation. On the basis of that fact, it might be concluded that there is a high degree of student satisfaction in Minnesota. To the contrary, sixty-two percent of Minnesota high school seniors told pollsters their schools did not challenge them. The state now permits public-school students to enroll early in postsecondary institutions of many kinds, including public vocational-technical institutes. In the first semester of this new program, these students had higher average grades than traditional freshmen (*Wall Street Journal*, Aug. 28, 1986, 14).

Ernest Boyer, former Secretary of the United States Office of Education, and chairman of the Carnegie Foundation for the Advancement of Teaching, advocated vouchers to pay for late-afternoon elective classes for students from poor families (*Newsweek*, Oct. 26, 1987, 75-76). Also, four governors came out in favor of vouchers, and a National Governors' Association task force on education supported more choices in schools, although not necessarily by vouchers. Change is in the offing!

Mark A. Kutner, Joel D. Sherman, and Mary F. Williams reviewed the trend toward assisting nongovernmental schools over the past twenty years, beginning with the Elementary and Secondary Education Act (ESEA) of 1965 which redefined the federal role in education and was the first federal program to contain provisions requiring federally funded services for private school students. The breakthrough which made possible congressional approval of ESEA came with an agreement between interest groups representing both public schools and religious organizations over a child-benefit approach to federal aid. The result of this agreement was that local school districts were required to make available to eligible private school students educational services paid for by the federal government (Kutner et al., 1986, 59).

Private enterprise in the health field also began to look at vouchers.

> Humana, which enrolled 500,000 patients in its group
> health program over the past two years, now plans to

offer such variations as a "voucher" plan for retirees covered by medicare. Says Humana's president, Wendell Cherry: "We think, [the voucher] is the system of the future." (Wilson and Cahan, *Business Week*, Jan. 13, 1986)

In the case of *Witters v. Washington Dept. of Services for the Blind*, the Supreme Court finally ruled January 27, 1986, on the question of whether an individual may use funds received from the government to attend a religious institution to study for the clergy, although thousands of GIs had done so without a challenge.

It said yes.

On the facts, it is inappropriate to view any state aid ultimately flowing to the Christian college as resulting from a *state* action sponsoring or subsidizing religion. Nor does the mere circumstance that petitioner has chosen to use neutrally available state aid to help pay for his religious education confer any message of state endorsement of religion. . . .

. . . . It is well settled that the Establishment Clause is not violated every time money previously in the possession of a State is conveyed to a religious institution. For example, a State may issue a paycheck to one of its employees, who may then donate all or part of that paycheck to a religious institution, all without constitutional barrier; and the State may do so even knowing that the employee so intends to dispose of his salary. It is equally well settled, on the other hand, that the State may not grant aid to a religious school, whether cash or in kind, where the effect of the aid is "that of a direct subsidy to the religious school" from the State . . . Aid may have that effect even though it takes the form of aid to students or parents . . . Washington's program is "made available generally without regard to the sectarian-nonsectarian, or public-nonpublic nature of the institution benefited" and is no way skewed toward religion.

Also, Washington State has an eight-year-old program for dropouts in which vouchers can be cashed at private institutions; in 1986 California began to implement a similar measure (Kelley 1986, 11).

Myron Lieberman suggested that:

> Private enterprise must do more than sell products to public and private schools. It must establish and operate schools . . . The private sector delivers other so-called public services more cheaply, and often better, than public agencies. I see no reason that it cannot do the same with education. (Lieberman 1986, 136)

John E. Chubb and Terry E. Moe, like so many before them, said that if government schools are going to be organized so they can make real improvements they may have to be allowed to function much like nongovernmental schools, with a large degree of teaching and professional autonomy.

> Effective control over schools would be transferred from government to the market. Government would . . . provide funding, in the form of vouchers allocated to parents. But virtually all the important decisions . . . would be taken out of the hands of politicians and administrators and given over to schools and their immediate clients: the students and their parents. (Chubb and Moe 1986, 34)

George Early, president of Learning Therapy Associates, believes

> the educational establishment is incapable of reform from within, and the voucher system seems our only hope of making a real impact on the situation. Putting the schools solidly into free enterprise undoubtedly would bring great improvement. (Early 1986)

Colorado Governor Richard Lamm, reporting on the findings of the National Governors' Association Task Force on

Parent Involvement and Choice, which he chaired, said it is ironic, in a land with one hundred cereals, two hundred different cars, and three hundred religious denominations from which to choose, that there isn't greater choice within the public school system, something people clearly want.

The task force, believing the present structure of public education cannot deal effectively with both the nation's diversity and its demand for compulsory education, recommended adopting legislation permitting families to select among public schools in their state and allowing 11th and 12th graders to attend accredited public postsecondary institutions, with tax funds following them, as in Minnesota (Lamm 1986, 211).

National columnist Neal Peirce was harsher:

Perhaps school boards are an idea whose time has come, and gone . . . At a minimum, the time is more than ripe for increased experimentation. School vouchers, for example . . . An heretical idea in "democratic" America? Perhaps . . . Rare is the school board that even toys with such innovative approaches. But the whirlwind of change has just started. (Peirce 1986)

Peter Brimelow supports choice in schooling:

There is no reason a private delivery system is incompatible with a government interest in fostering education. After all, Washington is in the food stamp business, not the supermarket business . . .

But, he laments,

. . . it won't happen soon. The education establishment is a confirmation of the public choice approach to economics for which James Buchanan was recently awarded the Nobel prize. Highly organized professional educators, sympathetic liberal legislators and a constituency of manipulable education consumers form a classic "iron triangle" that has proved impervious to reform. (Brimelow 1986, 76)

In Washington the Reagan Administration reintroduced its proposal to convert funds for remedial education of disadvantaged youth to vouchers, this time on a voluntary basis. The $3.9 billion program would provide about $800 for each of the five million eligible students.

However, the proposal could have targeted the remedial money to poor schools at the expense of some middle- and upper-income neighborhoods. Given that the latter two categories have much more political clout than the former, its chance of passage was further weakened (*The Patriot*, Dec. 30, 1986, A4).

With the Reagan Administration being followed by that of George Bush, however, continuing presidential support of vouchers and family choice was assured for the immediate future. This was demonstrated when the education summit conference of governors, called together by President Bush in late September 1989, included choice as one of the proposals it endorsed.

The words of Laura Hersh Salganik, written in 1981, still have merit:

> Since a true voucher system with nonpublic options and a workable information system has never been tried in the U.S., there is no direct evidence about what the education marketplace would be like . . . the paradox of universal, compulsory, state controlled schooling is that so long as we insist upon it, we cannot learn whether we need it, what we need it for, how it does whatever we suppose it does, or what might, if anything, better take its place. (Salganik 1981, 24)

Until funding from some source permits a fair trial of vouchers, their possible impact will not be known. Supporters should not, however, be disheartened. The ongoing debate is surely to some degree responsible for developments in Minnesota, the position of the National Governors' Association, alternative schools, and other movements in the direction of choice.

The urgency of the situation was dramatically illustrated in 1989 when the courts of Kentucky and Texas found their present system of providing education to be unconstitutional. In Kentucky the court said that meant the entire system—the school districts and school boards, the state department of education, as well as the funding mechanism.

In both states the court called for a very tight deadline to create an alternate, and acceptable, system. What that might be is still far from being determined as this volume was being prepared for press; but these cases bring the number of such court decisions at the state level to ten since *Serrano I* in California in 1971; choice is already on the scene, or being seriously considered, in twenty states; consideration in Kentucky is being given to ideas that were previously unacceptable in public debate; and the chances of a real restructuring of public schooling, including the possibility of an expanded use of vouchers, are perhaps greater than they have ever been.

The final step may yet be taken.

12

Summing Up:
The Idea That Will Not Die

Whether called "tuition vouchers," "education vouchers," "family choice," or described but given no name, the proposal to fund education by supporting students rather than institutions has been with us for more than two hundred years. While it is not the standard in basic education, both supporters and working models have been growing in recent years.

The most extensive example is the GI Bill, adopted as part of the Servicemen's Readjustment Act of 1944, which came about despite much opposition from the higher education community, the prime beneficiary of the plan. This Bill has shown the value of the idea, as have the many state and federal student grant programs since that time.

In basic education, too, the voucher approach has been making inroads. Although it has a history prior to World War II, its use has become more common since then, both in the United States—especially in New England—and elsewhere. England in 1945, Canadian provinces in the 1960s and 1970s, and Australia in the 1970s are but a few of the examples of progress that we have noted.

While Americans pride themselves on their social conscience and concern for the individual, other nations have often been in the forefront of establishing social programs. For example, Social Security was introduced in the United States in the 1930s, generations after its initiation in other industrialized nations. Even the autocratic regime of Bismarck's Prussia established such a program in the nineteenth century.

It is also a fact that most western democracies permit more choice in education than does the United States, this being the only industrial democracy that does not routinely aid nonpublic schools. The pity, as Chester E. Finn, Jr., wrote in the Foreword, is that research demonstrates the effectiveness of educational choice, especially for students of lower socioeconomic status, those for whom schooling is least successful.

That much of the educational establishment opposes even limited testing of vouchers, or other forms of educational choice, is not surprising. To reiterate what I have already said earlier, professions are rarely changed from within. Experts are experts of the status quo, of what *is* rather than what can be or what should be. They benefit from the status quo, or think they do, and they don't want to risk losing what they have, for promises of a better way. It shouldn't be surprising that this opposition is more apparent from the spokespersons for the organizations than from individual members.

In the early stages of the contemporary debate, in 1970, 43 percent of school administrators favored vouchers, as did 45 percent of the teachers, though this dropped to 20 percent for administrators a year later, after they had heard from their organizational leaders.

Teachers have shown more independence in their views. The percentage of their support for choice remains higher and, in many cities, 20 percent, 30 percent, or more of those with school-age children send them to nongovernment schools.

Students and parents have even stronger feelings. One survey showed high school juniors and seniors preferred to have vouchers by a two-to-one margin

In the 1986 Gallup Poll on education, 51 percent of public-school parents supported vouchers, to 41 percent opposed. Nonpublic-school parents registered a 64 to 28 approval rating

So why doesn't it happen?

The answers are many, most of which are typical of any proposal for significant change.

Opponents are well organized, in a relatively few large

groups, almost all with Washington headquarters and part of a common community. It also is easier to block change than to bring it about.

Supporters, if organized at all, belong to many, mostly small, groups, scattered across the country. They also are less unified in their support. Not all voucher proposals are the same, and some supporters seem to want their version or none at all.

As Milton Friedman has indicated, while a standard voucher might be second-place to a compensatory one by which students with special needs receive a voucher worth more than the standard amount, it would stand a greater chance of being adopted and would still be superior to the present arrangement.

The present system also has the advantage of at least being known, "warts and all." The proposed system is full of promise to its supporters, but seems to its detractors to present potential dangers, and fear of the unknown is always a potent factor in human affairs.

Politically—and this does come down to a political question—public officials find little if any profit to be had by being much ahead of public opinion in any area of life.

Further, many of the voices on both sides of the argument show little knowledge of the substance or history of the idea, or of examples that might be studied. In such an exchange of biases, prejudices, or otherwise predetermined positions, defenders of the status quo have the advantage.

Many supporters of vouchers also seem not so much to be really committed to educational choice and/or student welfare as they seem to be motivated by anti-teacher and anti-public school feelings or by an interest to get money for their own projects. While these more narrow views may be valid for some supporters, the general public is better off being persuaded that the goal of the proposed change is itself valid and of extensive value to the whole community.

Another difficulty arises because the idea has become associated in recent years with Republican and conservative causes, in contrast to most of its history, in which it had no particular ideological coloration. The major attention in recent

U.S. history began with the Office of Economic Opportunity proposal of 1970, during the Nixon Administration, and the resultant Alum Rock Project during the Nixon and Ford years. This has been followed by support from the Reagan Administration, both philosophically and with specific proposals to the 99th and 100th Congresses to convert Title I/Chapter I funds to voucher projects. That support has continued with the presidency of George Bush. The result has been for liberals and Democrats at the national level to run for cover instead of studying and supporting the idea as they might otherwise have done.

Sen. Daniel Patrick Moynihan (D.-N.Y.) is one prominent national Democrat who takes exception to the view of his colleagues. As he has pointed out, for most of its history the voucher idea has been more than acceptable to liberals, and "if it prevails only as a conservative cause, it will have been a great failure of American liberalism not to have seen the essentially liberal nature of this pluralist proposition." (Moynihan 1981, 84).

It is also unfortunately true that many Americans lack a basic commitment to democracy and pluralism, despite slogans, rhetoric, ceremonies, and protestations to the contrary. If we respect each other's opinions, believe in individual freedom, cherish diversity, and have confidence in each other, why do we fear letting parents determine the course of their children's education?

Why do we apparently believe that Americans will not bring up their children to be "good citizens" unless we coerce them, and ourselves in the process, to accept a standardized, government-approved and regulated education?

Most professed advocates of education are in actuality only advocates of schooling. There are supporters of government schools and supporters of nongovernment schools. What is too often lacking are supporters of education, those concerned with our children and their education, rather than with specific institutions. So it is that we have compulsory schooling, not compulsory education, as the phrase usually has it. There is no requirement that citizens be educated, as millions of

high school dropouts and hundreds of thousands of function-
ally illiterate graduates each year demonstrate.

Few words on this subject have been as powerful or as
eloquent as those of U.S. Supreme Court Associate Justice
Robert H. Jackson, writing for the Court in 1943 in *West Virginia
Board of Education v. Barnette,* the still-controversial decision
that requiring students to salute the flag and pledge allegiance
is a violation of their First Amendment rights:

> Struggles to coerce uniformity of sentiment in support
> of some end thought essential to their time and coun-
> try have been waged by many good as well as by evil
> men. As governmental pressure toward unity be-
> comes greater, so strife becomes more bitter as to
> whose unity it shall be. Probably no deeper division of
> our people could proceed from any provocation than
> from finding it necessary to choose what doctrine and
> whose program public educational officials shall
> compel youth to unite in embracing. Ultimate futility
> of such attempts to compel coherence is the lesson of
> every such effort.... Those who begin coercive elimi-
> nation of dissent soon find themselves exterminating
> dissenters. Compulsory unification of opinion achieves
> only the unanimity of the graveyard.

In a system of governmental schooling it is unavoidably
"necessary to choose what doctrine and whose program public
educational officials shall compel youth to unite in embracing,"
and the nearly half-century since Jackson penned those words
has seen the gradual unfolding of the divisiveness he foresaw
proceeding from such an effort.

This is demonstrated by the exponential increase in educational litigation before the Supreme Court. From the Court's
first session, Feb. 1, 1790, until 1908, it decided 6 such cases.
From 1909-1928, it handed down 5 decisions; from 1929-1948,
14; from 1949-1965, 40; and from 1966-1984, 140 (Karier 1986,
407).

Whether it is because of growing social unrest, or of an

ongoing debate, or of developments in other nations, or of the growing trend to "privatization" of government functions, or because of any combination thereof, the movement toward educational choice, with or without vouchers, seems to be building momentum.

Former Delaware governor Pete du Pont, speaking to University of Iowa law students, while campaigning for the Republican presidential nomination, proposed replacing government schools with vouchers. the value of which would be equal to the per-pupil assessments in their school districts. He argued, as have others, that this would promote competition and better student performance. [*Evening News* (Harrisburg), September 23, 1987]. He is apparently the first candidate for the presidential nomination ever to openly state such a position.

As noted in chapter 11, four governors indicated support for vouchers. At President George Bush's education summit conference of governors in September 1989, support was shown for choice among public schools. Minnesota became the first state of a growing number of states to allow every student to attend any of its public schools.

In any event, the end of the voucher debate has not yet come. It may continue until some form of the proposal is adopted, or other great reforms negate the need currently perceived by so many.

In 1990 Wisconsin became the first state to adopt a tuition voucher plan for public school students to use at secular private schools. Under this new law 1,000 disadvantaged students in Madison, which has 97,000 students in its public schools may receive up to $2,500 each to attend other nonreligious institutions. This law was new at press time and had not been implemented.

In mid-1990, the New Jersey Supreme Court became the latest to rule unconstitutional its state's manner of financing public education. Similar suits are pending in a number of other states and the process is getting underway in Pennsylvania where, as this book goes to press, 70 school districts have joined together to take such action, and others are expected to follow. The author is Executive Director of the Association which is serving as the catalyst for the action.

Dissatisfaction with the present system is growing from within the educaional establishment, as well as from without.

The question, perhaps, is not so much whether you would prefer to have educational choice for yourself, as a student or parent—a question to which most people would probably reply yes—but whether you are prepared to grant that choice to others. So far, despite the ongoing plurality or majority of support in public opinion polls, our collective answer has generally been no.

That may be changing.

Appendix

As Alexis de Tocqueville remarked a century and a half ago, citizens of the United States are inclined to form associations. Today there are countless, and continually changing, numbers of them. On vouchers alone quite a list could be assembled of groups with some interest in the topic.

The following is therefore by no means exhaustive. Nor have all the organizations necessarily taken a stand for or against vouchers. It is presented only as a starting point for those who wish to pursue the matter.

There are also many individuals active in this area, many of whom are cited in this book, with or without an affiliation with one of the following. They have not been included here, nor have the officers of the organizations, because the mobility of Americans guarantees that the addresses of any such list would be inaccurate before the book appears and because there was no wish to unduly interfere with their privacy.

In the present political environment a disproportionate percentage of these groups tend to be conservative. As indicated in the text, vouchers have not historically been aligned with any particular political philosophy but liberal organizations have become hesitant to endorse current voucher efforts for a number of reasons, not all of which have to do with the merits of the proposal itself. This is an unfortunate reality. With those caveats, therefore, here are some possibilities:

American Assn of Christian
   Schools
Box 1088
10195 Main St., Suite P
Fairfield, VA 22030
703/273-1164

American Coalition for
   Traditional Values
122 C St., N.W., Suite 850
Washington, D.C. 20001
202/628-2967

171

American Conservative Union
38 Ivy St., S.E.
Washington, D.C. 20003
202/546-6555

American Enterprise Institute
  for Public Policy Research
1150 17th St., N.W.
Washington, D.C. 20036
202/862-5800

Assn for Christian Schools
Box 35096
Houston, TX 77035
713/666-3111

Assn for Public Justice
806 15th St., N.W., Suite 218
Washington, D.C. 20005
202/737-2110

Assn of Christian Schools
  International
731 Beech Blvd.
La Habra, CA 90631

Baptist Joint Committee on
  Public Affairs
200 Maryland Ave., N.E.
Washington, D.C. 20002
202/544-4226

Brookings Institution
1775 Mass. Ave., N.W.
Washington, D.C. 20036
202/797-6000

The Catholic League for
  Religious and Civil Rights
1100 West Wells St.
Milwaukee, WI 53233

CATO Institute
224 Second St., N.E.
Washington, D.C. 20003
202/546-0200

Christian Schools Internatl
3350 E. Paris Ave.
Grand Rapids, MI 49508
616/957-1070

Citizens for Educational
  Freedom
1611 N. Kent St.
Arlington, VA 22209
703/524-1991

Clearinghouse on Educational
  Choice
1611 N. Kent St.
Arlington, VA 22209
703/524-1556

Committee for Public
  Education and Religious
  Liberty
c/o UPA
70 Lafayette St.
New York, N.Y. 10013
212/964-8847

Conservative Alliance
1001 Prince St.
Alexandria, VA 22314
703/684-3980

Conservative Caucus
450 Maple Ave. E.
Vienna, VA
703/893-1550

Council for American Private
Education
Room 822
1625 Eye St., N.W.
Washington, D.C. 20006
202/659-0016

Council for Educational
Freedom in America
2105 Wintergreen Ave.
Forestville, MD 20747
301/336-1585

Educational Freedom Fd
20 Parkland
Glendale
St. Louis, MO 63122
314/966-3485.

First Amendment Research
Institute
1145 19th St., N.W.
Suite 717
Washington, D.C. 20036
202/857-3280

Free Congress Research and
Education Foundation
721 Second St., N.E.
Washington, D.C. 20002
202/546-3004

Freedom Council
Virginia Beach, VA 23466
804/420-0773

Heritage Education and
Review Organization
Box 202
Jarretsville, MD 21084
301/557-9846

Heritage Foundation
214 Mass. Ave., N.E.
Washington, D.C. 20002
202/546-4400

Home Education Resource
Center
Box 124
Mt. Vernon, NH 03057

Hudson Institute
Herman Kahn Center
5395 Emerson Way
Box 26-919
Indianapolis, IN 46226

Institute for Liberty and
Community
Concord, VT 05824
802/695-2555

Natl Assn for Legal Support of
Alternative Schools
Box 2823
Santa Fe, New Mexico 87501
505/471-6928

Natl Catholic Conference for
Interracial Justice
1200 Varnum St., N.E.
Washington, D.C. 20017
202/529-6480

Natl Catholic Education Assn
Suite 100, 1077 30th St., N.W.
Washington, D.C. 20007
202/337-6232

The Natl Center for
  Privatization
Box 1998
Wichita, Kansas 67201-1998
316/687-4000

Natl Coalition of Advocates
  for Students
76 Summer St., 3d Flr.
Boston, MA 02110
617/357-8507

Natl Coalition of Alternative
  Community Schools
Box 378, RD 1
Glenmoore, PA 19343
215/458-5138

Natl Coalition of Title I/
  Chapter I Parents
National Parent Center
1314 14th St., N.W., Suite 6
Washington, D.C., 20005
202/483-8822

Natl Pro-Family Coalition
721 Second St., N.E.
Washington, D.C. 20002
202/546-5342

Parents' Alliance to Protect
  Our Children
44 E. Tacoma Ave.
Latrobe, PA 15650
412/459-6347

Parents Rights Organization
12571 Northwinds Drive
St. Louis, MO 63146
314/434-4171

Privatization Council
30 Rockefeller Center
Suite 3755
New York, NY 10112
212/247-1872

Public School Incentives
1885 University Ave.
St. Paul, MN 55104

The Sequoia Institute
3353 Bradshaw Road
Suite 121
Sacramento, CA 95827
916/353-5675

Thomas J. White Educational
  Foundation
940 West Port Plaza
St. Louis, MO 63146
314/878-0400

U.S. Catholic Conference,
  Education
1312 Mass. Ave., N.W.
Washington, D.C. 20005
202/659-6718

Bibliography

The following bibliography is the product of my research in the field of education during the past nineteen years and reflects my direct involvement in education and schooling for many more years than that. For those seeking a somewhat shorter yet worthwhile basic program, I would especially recommend three sources:

First, for an understanding of "a place called school," there is perhaps no better single source than John I. Goodlad's work of that name. *A Place Called School* is one of the most thorough and balanced evaluations that anyone has produced.

Second, for an understanding of vouchers and the arguments in their behalf, the work of John E. Coons and his colleagues stands out. *Education by Choice: The Case For Family Control*, written by Coons and his longtime co-worker Stephen D. Sugarman, is suggested as a starting point because it is a work of depth produced after both the Serrano decisions and the Alum Rock project.

Finally—and in some ways the most intriguing because he almost has the field to himself—there is Stephen Arons's *Compelling Belief* with its provocative thesis about the essential need to separate school and state. To these I would add any of the following sources, depending on your particular interests and needs.

ALLEN, JAMES E., JR.
December 1969. "Overview Role of Federal Government in Education Defined." In *Pennsylvania School Journal*. Pp. 80-82. Harrisburg, Pa.: Pennsylvania State Education Assn.

ALONZO, BRAULIO
1968. *NEA Convention Proceedings.*

AMERICA
June 20, 1970. "The Jencks Tuition Voucher Plan." Pp. 644-45.

April 5, 1986. "Questions for American Education." P. 157.

ARONS, STEPHEN
February 1971. "Equity, Option and Vouchers." *Teacher College Record.* Pp. 337-63.

1972. "The Peaceful Use of Education Vouchers." In *Educational Vouchers: Concepts and Controversies.* Ed. George LaNoue. New York: Teachers College Press.

Nov. 6, 1973. "Compulsory Education: America in Mississippi." *Saturday Review.*

February 1976. "The Separation of School and State: *Pierce* Reconsidered." *Harvard Educational Review.* Pp. 76-104.

1983. *Compelling Belief.* New York: McGraw-Hill Book Co.

ASCIK, THOMAS R.
1985. "The Courts and Education." In *A New Agenda for Education.* Ed. Eileen M. Gardner. Pp. 59-77. Washington, D.C.: The Heritage Foundation.

BAIDA, PETER
Winter 1985/86. "Confesssions of a Reluctant Yuppie." In *American Scholar.* Pp. 45-54.

BANE, MARY JO
February 1971. "Essay Reviews." *Harvard Educational Review.*

BASS, GAIL V.
1978. *A Study in American Education,* Volume 1: *District Policies and the Implementation of Change.* Santa Monica, CA: The Rand Corporation.

BECKER, G. S.
March 24, 1986. "Give All Parents a Say in Choosing Schools."
Business Week. P. 19.

BENDINER, ROBERT
1969. *The Politics of Schools, A Crisis in Self-Government.* New
York: Harper & Row.

BENNETT, WILLIAM J.
Dec. 11, 1985. "Vouchers a good way to improve education."
USA Today. P. A10.

BENSON, CHARLES, and THOMAS A. SHANNON
1972. *Schools Without Property Taxes: Hope or Illusion?* Bloomington, Indiana: The Phi Delta Kappa Educational Foundation.

BEREITER, CARL
Dec. 1973. "Must We Educate?" *Phi Delta Kappan.* Pp. 233-36.

BERENGER, RALPH D.
June 1975. COMPACT MAGAZINE. P. 5.

BESTOR, ARTHUR
1953. *Educational Wastelands.* Urbana, Illinois: University of
Illinois Press.

BINZEN, PETER
1970. *Whitetown, U.S.A.* New York: Random House.

BIRMINGHAM, JOHN, ED.
1970. *Our Time Is Now: Notes From the High School Underground.*
New York: Praeger.

BLANCHARD, EVERARD
1975. *A New System of Education.* Homewood, Illinois: ETC
Publications.

BLUM, VIRGIL
1958. *Freedom of Choice in Education.* New York: Macmillan.

BLUM, VIRGIL (cont.)
>   March 15, 1974. "The Supreme Court and Religion." *Vital
>   Speeches of the Day.* (So. Carolina: City News Publisher). Pp.
>   337-41.
>
>   April 1, 1978. "Quality Education for Inner-City Minorities:
>   Education Vouchers." *Vital Speeches of the Day.* (So. Carolina:
>   City News Publisher). Pp. 362-66.
>
>   1981. "Why Inner-City Families Send Their Children to Private
>   Schools: An Empirical Study." In *Private Schools and The Public
>   Good.* Ed. Edward McGlynn Gaffney, Jr. Pp. 17-24. Notre
>   Dame, Indiana: University of Notre Dame Press.
>
>   1986. *Quest for Religious Freedom.* Milwaukee, Wisconsin: The
>   Catholic League for Religious and Civil Rights.

BOULDING, KENNETH E.
>   1973. *Challenge to Leadership, Managing in a Changing World.* The
>   Conference Board. New York: The Free Press.
>
>   Sept. 1976. "Publicly Supported, Universally Available Educa-
>   tion and Equality." In *Phi Delta Kappan.* Pp. 36-41.

BOYER, ERNEST L.
>   1983. *High School.* New York: Harper & Row.

BRAUN, ROBERT J.
>   1972. *Teachers and Power: The Story of the American Federation of
>   Teachers.* New York: Simon & Schuster.

BRIDGE, R. GARY
>   1977. "Citizen Choice in Public Services: Voucher Systems."
>   In *Alternatives for Delivering Public Services.* Ed. E. S. Savas.
>   Boulder, Colorado: Westview Press.
>
>   1978. "Information Imperfections: The Achilles' Heel of Enti-
>   tlement Plans." In *School Review,* 86: 504-29.

BRIDGE, R. GARY AND JULIE BLACKMAN
>   1978. *A Study of Alternatives in American Education.* Vol. IV:
>   *Family Choice in Schooling.* Santa Monica, Calif.: The Rand
>   Corp.

BRIMELOW, PETER
>   1985. "Competition for Public Schools." In *The Great School
>   Debate: Which Way For American Education?* Ed. Beatrice and
>   Ronald Gross. Pp. 345-53. New York: Simon and Schuster,
>   Inc.
>
>   Dec. 29, 1986. "Are we spending too much on education?"
>   *Forbes.* Pp. 72-76.

BROZEN, YALE, and ROMAN L. WEIL
>   1971. *The Voucher System.* 15pp. Washington, D.C.: American
>   Conservative Union.

CALIFORNIA ASSEMBLY REPUBLICAN CAUCUS
>   1979. *Background Material on the Family Choice Initiative.*
>   Sacramento, California.

CALIFORNIA COALITION FOR FAIR SCHOOL FINANCE
>   1979a. *A Description of the Family Choice in Education Initiative.*
>   Menlo Park, Calif.
>
>   1979b. *Testimony on the Family Choice in Education Initiative.*
>   Menlo Park, Calif.

CALIFORNIA SUPREME COURT
>   Aug. 30, 1971. *Serrano v. Priest.* 487 PAC 1241 (*Serrano I*).
>
>   Dec. 30, 1976. *Serrano v. Priest.* 557 PAC 929 (*Serrano II*).

CAMPBELL, ROALD F., LAVERN L. CUNNINGHAM, and RODERICK F.
>   McPHEE
>   1965. *The Organization and Control of American Schools.*
>   Columbus, Ohio: Charles E. Merrill Publishing Co.

CARNEGIE COMMISSION ON HIGHER EDUCATION
>   April 1971. *The Capitol and the Campus: A Report and
>   Recommendations.* New York: McGraw-Hill Book Co.
>
>   February 1972. *Institutional Aid: A Report and Recommendations.*
>   New York: McGraw-Hill Book Co.
>
>   June 1972a. *The More Effective Use of Resources.* New York:
>   McGraw-Hill Book Co.

CARNEGIE COMMISSION ON HIGHER EDUCATION (cont.)
June 1972b. *Reform on Campus: A Report and Recommendations.*
New York: McGraw-Hill Book Co.

1973. *Priorities for Action: Final Report.* New York: McGraw-Hill Book Co.

April 1973. *Governance of Higher Education: A Report and Recommendations.* New York: McGraw-Hill Book Co.

August 1973. *Continuity and Discontinuity: Higher Education and the Schools.* New York: McGraw-Hill Book Co.

1975. *Sponsored Research of the Carnegie Commission.* New York: McGraw-Hill Book Co.

CARNEGIE TASK FORCE
June 29, 1987. *A Nation Prepared: Teachers for the 21st Century.* In *Education Week.* P. C3.

CARR, RAY A., and GERALD C. HAYWARD
February 1970. "Education by Chit: An Examination of Voucher Proposals." In *Education and Urban Society.*

CENTER FOR THE STUDY OF PUBLIC POLICY (CAMBRIDGE, MASS.)
December 1970. *Education Vouchers: A Report on Financing Elementary Education by Grants to Parents.*

CHAMBERLAIN, JOHN
May 6, 1970. "How about educational vouchers?" Harrisburg, Pa.: *The Evening News.*

CHAMBERS, JOHN
March/April 1978. "An Analysis of School Size Under a Voucher System." In *Educational Evaluation and Policy Analysis,* Vol. 3, No. 2. Pp. 29-40.

CHRISTIAN CENTURY
Dec. 2, 1970. Letters to the Editor. Pp. 1460-61.

CHUBB, JOHN E., and TERRY E. MOE
June 24, 1986. "Higher Teacher Pay Doesn't Make the Grade." In *The Wall Street Journal.* P. 34.

CLARK, KENNETH B.
1969. "Alternative Public School Systems." In *Equal Education Opportunity*. Cambridge, Mass: Harvard University Press.

CLAYTON, A. STAFFORD
Sept. 1970. "Vital Questions, Minimal Responses." *Phi Delta Kappan*.

COHEN, DAVID K.
Nov. 1978. "Reforming School Politics." *Harvard Educational Review*. Pp. 429-47.

COHEN, DAVID K., and ELEANOR FARRAR
1984. "Power to the Parents?—The Story of Education Vouchers." In *The Public Interest on Education*. Ed. Nathan Glazer. Pp. 241-66. Lanham, Md.: University Press of America.

COLEMAN, JAMES S.
1977. "Introduction: Choice in Education." In *Parents, Teachers, and Children*. S.F., CA.: Institute for Contemporary Studies.

1980. "Choice in Education." In *The Analysis of Educational Productivity*. Ed. Charles Bidwell and Douglas Windham. Volume 2, *Issues in Macroanalysis*. Cambridge, Mass.: Ballinger.

COLEMAN JAMES S., THOMAS HOFFER, and SALLY KILGORE
1982. *High School Achievement: Public, Catholic and Private Schools Compared*. New York: Basic Books.

COLEMAN, JAMES S., and THOMAS HOFFER
1987. *Public and Private High Schools*. New York: Basic Books.

COMMITTEE ON ECONOMIC DEVELOPMENT (CED)
March 1976. *Improving Productivity in State and Local Government*. New York.

June 24, 1987. *Investing in Our Children* (Policy Committee). Quoted in *Education Week*. P. C3.

COMPACT
Spring 1976. P. 11. Denver: Ed. Commission of the States.

CONANT, JAMES BRYANT
1961. *Slums and Suburbs.* New York: McGraw-Hill Book Co.

THE CONFERENCE BOARD
1973. *Challenge to Leadership, Managing in a Changing World.*
New York: The Free Press.

COOK, JAMES
March 24, 1986. "The knack . . . and how to get it." In *Forbes.*
Pp. 56-66.

COONS, JOHN E.
Mar. 16, 1970. "Recreating the Family's Role in Education." In
Inequality in Education. Harvard Center for Law and Education.

Sept. 1976. "Law and the Sovereigns of Childhood." *Phi Delta
Kappan.* Pp. 19-24.

1980. "Can Education be Equal and Excellent?" In *School
Finance Policies and Practices—The 1980s: A Decade of Conflict.*
Ed. James W. Guthrie. Pp. 131-42. Cambridge, Mass.: Ballinger
Publishing Co.

1981. "Making Schools Public." In *Private Schools and the Public
Good.* Ed. Edward McGlynn Gaffney, Jr. Pp. 91-105. Notre
Dame, Indiana: University of Notre Dame Press.

February 1985. "A Question of Access." *Independent School.* Pp.
9-20.

COONS JOHN E., and STEPHEN D. SUGARMAN
1971 *Family Choice in Education: A Model State System for
Vouchers.* Berkeley, Calif.: Institute of Governmental Studies,
University of California.

1978. Education by Choice: The Case for Family Control.
Berkeley, Calif.:University of California Press.

COONS, JOHN E., WILLIAM H. CLUNE III, and STEPHEN D. SUGARMAN
April 1969. "Educational Opportunity: A Workable Constitu-
tional Test for State Finanacial Structures." In *California Law
Review,* vol. 57, #2. Berkeley, Calif.: Law Review Inc.

COONS, JOHN E., WILLIAM H. CLUNE III, and STEPHEN D. SUGARMAN
      (cont.)
   1970. *Private Wealth and Public Education.* Cambridge, Mass:
   The Belknap Press of Harvard University Press.

   1972. "Reslicing the School Pie." In *Educational Vouchers:
   Concepts and Controversies.* Ed. George LaNoue. New York:
   Teachers College Press.

COX, PATRICK
   Dec. 11, 1985. "Let's have vouchers for everybody." *USA
   Today.* P. A10.

CRARY, RYLAND, W.
   1969. *Humanizing the School.* New York: Alfred A. Knopf.

CREMIN, LAWRENCE
   1965. *The Genius of American Education.* New York: Vintage
   Books.

CROMLEY, RAY
   Oct. 31, 1985. *"New Education Ways Tried."* Williamsport, Pa.:
   Sun-Gazette. P. 13.

CUNNINGHAM, ROBERT L.
   (n.d.) *Education: Free and Public.* Wichita, Kansas: Center for
   Independent Education.

CYERT, RICHARD M.
   Oct. 10, 1974. *The Market Approach to Higher Education.* Paper
   presented to the 57th Annual Meeting of the American Council
   on Education, San Diego, Calif.

DAHL, JOHN A., MARVIN LASER, ROBERT S. CATHCART, and FRED S.
      MARCUS, EDS.
   1964. *Student, School & Society.* San Francisco: Chandler Publishing Co.

D'ALESSIO, EDWARD R.
   1981. Preface. In *Private Schools and the Public Good.* Ed. Edward McGlynn Gaffney, Jr. Notre Dame, Indiana: University
   of Notre Dame Press. Pp. x-xii.

DENNISON, GEORGE
1969. *The Lives of Children.* New York: Random House.

DIVOKY, DIANE, ED.
1969. *How Old Will You Be in 1984?* New York: Avon Books.

DONALDSON, GORDON A., JR.
1977. *Education Vouchers in New Hampshire: An Attempt at Free Market Educational Reform.* Newton, Mass: Leinwand Assocs.

DONALDSON, GORDON A., Jr., and WILLIAM WEBER
1977. *Vouchers in East Hartford, Connecticut and New Hampshire: A Summary.* Newton, Mass: Leinwand Associates.

DOYLE, DENIS P.
1977. "The Politics of Choice: A View From the Bridge." In *Parents, Teachers, and Children: Prospects for Choice in Education.* San Francisco: Institute for Contemporary Studies.

Dec. 30, 1979. "A New Decade for U.S. Education: Who Pays, Who Gains, Who Loses?" *Los Angeles Times.*

June 15, 1980. "Implications of the Shift from Public Education." *The Washington Star.*

Sept. 1980. "Public Policy and Private Education." *Phi Delta Kappan.* Pp. 16-19.

1981. "Public Funding and Private Schooling: The State of Descriptive and Analytical Research." In *Private Schools and the Public Good.* Ed. Edward McGlynn Gaffney, Jr. Pp. 71-78. Notre Dame, Indiana: University of Notre Dame Press.

EARLY, GEORGE H.
July 11, 1986. *The Wall Street Journal.* Letter to the Editor. P. 21.

EDUCATION U.S.A.
October 12, 1970. "Public Attitude Toward School Disclosed." P. 31.

March 8, 1976. "Education Vouchers: Dead or Dying." P. 163.

EDUCATIONAL VOUCHERS: SYMPOSIUM VIEWS
December 1974 (reprint). Distributed by the Catholic League for Religious and Civil Rights. 1100 West Wells St., Milwaukee, Wisconsin 53233. Reprinted with permission in *Freedom in Education*. Citizens for Educational Freedom, 15th St. and New York Ave., N.W., Washington, D.C.

ENCARNATION, DENNIS J.
1983. "Public Finance and Regulation of Nonpublic Education: Retrospect and Prospect." In *Public Dollars for Private Schools*. Ed. Thomas James and Henry M. Levin. Pp.175-95. Phila.: Temple University Press.

EURICH, ALVIN C.
1969. *Reforming American Education*. New York: Harper & Row.

1970. *High School 1980*. New York: Pitman Publishing Corp.

THE EVENING NEWS (Harrisburg, Pa.)
Sept. 23, 1987. "Dupont Urges Voucher System for All Schools." P. A7.

FANTINI, MARIO D.
Dec. 11, 1985. "Our public schools are rigid, inflexible." *USA Today*. P. A10.

FARMER, JAMES
May 4, 1970. *Presidents' Notes*. Harrisburg, Pa: Pa. State Education Assn.

FENSTERMACHER, GARY
Winter 1979. "Deciders and Providers of Schooling." *California Journal of Teacher Education*. Pp. 23-40.

FEUER, LEWIS S.
1969. *The Conflict of Generations*. New York: Basic Books Inc.

FINCH, LEW.
September 1985. "Con: Public School Vouchers Jeopardize Equal Opportunity." *The School Administrator*. Pp. 11-12.

FINN, CHESTER E., JR.
Winter 1982. "Choice as Justice." In *IFG Policy Notes*. Stanford Calif.: Institute for Research on Educational Finance and Governance, Stanford University.

Nov./Dec. 1985. "Chester Finn Has Nine Big Ideas for the Next Ten Years." *Instructor*. Pp. 90-92.

FISCHER, JOHN H.
Sept. 19, 1970. "Who Needs Schools." In *Saturday Review*.

FISH, KENNETH L.
1970. *Conflict and Dissent in the High School*. New York: Bruce Publishing Co.

FLESCH, RUDOLF
1955. *Why Johnny Can't Read*. New York: Perennial Library.

THE FORD FOUNDATION
September 1974. *Matters of Choice*. A Report on Alternative Schools. New York: Ford Foundation.

FOWLER, FRANCES C.
January 1987. "The French Experience with Public Aid to Private Schools." In *Phi Delta Kappan*. Pp. 356-59.

FRIEDMAN, DAVID
n.d. (1971?) *Toward a Competitive School System*. Wichita, Kansas: Center for Independent Education.

FRIEDMAN, MILTON
1955. "The Role of Government in Education." In *Economics and the Public Interest*. Ed. Robert A. Solo. Pp. 123-44. New Brunswick, N.J.: Rutgers University Press.

1962. *Capitalism and Freedom*. Chicago: The University of Chicago Press.

1975. *There's No Such Thing as a Free Lunch*. LaSalle, Ill.: Open Court.

1984. *Tyranny of the Status Quo*. New York: Harcourt Brace Jovanovich.

Fuchs, Estelle
    Aug. 16, 1969. "The Free Schools of Denmark." *Saturday
    Review*. Pp. 44-46.

Fuentes, Luis
    June 1976. "Community Control Did Not Fail in New York: It
    Wasn't Tried." *Phi Delta Kappan*. Pp. 692-95.

The Futurist
    Nov./Dec. 1987. "Global Privatization." Pp. 39-40.

Gallup, Alex M.
    September 1986. "The 18th Annual Gallup Poll of the Public's
    Attitudes Toward the Public Schools." In *Phi Delta Kappan*. Pp.
    43-59.

Gallup, George H.
    Sept. 1971. "The Third Annual Survey of the Public's Attitude
    Toward the Public Schools." *Phi Delta Kappan*. Pp. 33-48.

    Sept. 1973. "Fifth Annual Poll of Public Attitudes Toward
    Education." *Phi Delta Kappan*. Pp. 38-51.

    Sept. 1983. "The 15th Annual Poll of the Public's Attitudes
    Toward the Public Schools." Phi Delta Kappan. Pp. 33-47.

Ganz, Mary
    Oct. 24, 1976. "Trial Voucher System Proves a Mixed Blessing
    to Schools." In *The Times-Picayune*, New Orleans, La., Section 3.
    P. 4.

Gardner, Eileen M., ed.
    1985. *A New Agenda for Education*. Washington, D.C.: The
    Heritage Foundation.

Garms, Walter I., James W. Guthrie, and Lawrence C. Pierce
    1978 *School Finance: The Economics and Politics of Public Educa-
    tion*. Englewood Cliffs, N.J.: Prentice-Hall Inc.

Gerson, Mark
    July 23, 1986. *The Chronicle of Higher Education*. P. 39.

GERWITZ, AARON SAMUEL
    1982. *The Economics of School Finance.* Cambridge, Mass:
    Ballinger Publishing Co.

GINZBERG, ELI
    February 1971. "The Economics of the Voucher System."
    Teacher College Record. Pp. 373-82.

GLAZER, NATHAN
    1977. "Public Education and American Pluralism." In *Parents,
    Teachers, and Children.* San Francisco: Institute for Contempo-
    rary Studies.

    1983. "The Future Under Tuition Tax Credits." In *Public
    Dollars for Private Schools.* Ed. Thomas James and Henry M.
    Levin. Pp. 87-100. Philadelphia: Temple University Press.

GLAZER, NATHAN, ED.
    1984. *The Public Interest on Education.* Lanham, Md: University
    Press of America Inc.

GLENNERSTER, HOWARD, and GAIL WILSON
    1970. *Paying for Private Schools.* London: University of London
    School of Economics and Political Science. Higher Education
    Res. Unit. Studies on education. Allen Lane, The Penguin
    Press.

GLINES, DONALD
    March 24-26, 1971. "Humane Year-Round Schools." In *Pro-
    ceedings of the 3rd National Seminar on Year-Round Education.* Pp.
    31a-g. Cocoa Beach, Fla.

GOLDBERG, KIRSTEN
    May 18, 1988. "Vermont's 'Tuitioning' Is Nation's Oldest
    Brand of Choice." In *Education Week.* Pp. 8-9.

GOLDMAN, L.
    January 1986. "The Time Has Come for Educational Divesti-
    ture." In *Education Digest.* Pp. 6-9.

GOODLAD, JOHN I.
    1984. *A Place Called School.* New York: McGraw-Hill Book Co.

GOODMAN, PAUL
1964. *Compulsory Mis-Education and the Community of Scholars.*
New York: Vintage Books.

1970. *New Reformation: Notes of a Neolithic Conservative.* New
York: Random House.

GOWIN, BOB
1981. *Educating.* Ithaca, New York: Cornell University Press.

GREELEY, REV. ANDREW M.
1981. "Catholic High Schools and Minority Students." In
Private Schools and the Public Good. Ed. Edward McGlynn
Gaffney, Jr. Pp. 6-16. Notre Dame, Ind: University of Notre
Dame Press.

GREER, COLIN
Nov. 15, 1969. "Public Schools: The Myth of the Melting Pot."
Saturday Review. Pp. 84-86.

GROSS, RONALD, and BEATRICE GROSS, EDS.
1969. *Radical School Reform.* New York: Simon & Schuster.

1985. *The Great School Debate.* New York: Simon & Schuster.

GUTHRIE, JAMES W., ED.
1980. *School Finance Policies and Practices /The 1980s: A Decade of
Conflict.* Cambridge, Mass: Ballinger Publishing Co.

HABERMAN, MARTIN
June 1986. "Licensing Teachers: Lessons from other
Professions." *Phi Delta Kappan.* Pp. 719-82.

HARRIS, SYDNEY
July 20, 1976. Harrisburg, Pa.: *The Patriot.* P. 14.

HART, LESLIE
1969. *The Classroom Disaster.* New York: Columbia Univ.
Teachers College Press.

HAVIGHURST, ROBERT J.
September 1970. "The Unknown Good: Education Vouchers."
Phi Delta Kappan. Pp. 52-53.

HAYEK, FRIEDRICH A., VON
> February 1975. In *Reason Magazine*. P. 10. Santa Monica: Reason Foundation.

HEALEY, ROBERT M.
> 1974. *The French Achievement, Private School Aid: A Lesson for America*. New York: Paulist Press.

HENNEBERGER, MELINDA
> August 13, 1986. "Small town in rural America knows how to think big." *The Philadelphia Inquirer*, A-3.

HENTOFF, MARGOT
> Sept. 19, 1970. "The Schools We Want: A Family Dialogue." *Saturday Review*.

HENTOFF, NAT
> 1977. *Does Anybody Give a Damn?* New York: Alfred A. Knopf.

HERNDON, JAMES
> 1968. *The Way It Spozed to Be*. New York: Simon & Schuster.

HEW (Health Education and Welfare)
> 1974. *Inside-Out: The Final Report and Recommendations of the Teachers National Field Task Force on the Improvement and Reform of American Education*. Washington, D.C.

HIRSCHOFF, MARY-MICHELL UPSON
> 1986. "Public Policy Toward Private Schools: A Focus on Parental Choice." *Private Education*. Ed. Daniel C. Levy. Pp. 33-56. New York: Oxford University Press.

HOLT, JOHN
> 1964. *How Children Fail*. New York: Dell Publishing Co., Inc.

> 1967. *How Children Learn*. New York: Pitman Publishing Corp.

> 1969. *The Underachieving School*. New York: Pitman Publishing Corp.

> 1970. *What Do I Do Monday?* New York: E. P. Dutton.

> 1974. *Escape From Childhood*. New York: E. P. Dutton.

HUBERMAN, MICHAEL
1974. "Learning, Democratizing, and Deschooling." In *Deschooling*. Ed. Ian Lister. Pp 46-58. Cambridge, England: Cambridge University Press.

HURLEY, RODGER
1969. *Poverty and Mental Retardation: A Causal Relationship*. New York: Random House.

ILLICH, IVAN
1971. *Deschooling Society*. New York: Harper & Row.

JACOBSON, ROBERT L.
Oct. 31, 1980. "Colorado Eyes Vouchers to Finance Higher Education." *The Chronicle of Higher Education*. Pp. 1, 4.

JAMES, ESTELLE
1986. "Public Subsidies for Private and Public Education: The Dutch Case." In *Private Education*. Ed. Daniel C. Levy. Pp. 113-57. New York: Oxford University Press.

JAMES, THOMAS
1983. "Questions About Educational Choice: An Argument from History." In *Public Dollars for Private Schools*. Ed. Thomas James and Henry M. Levin. Pp. 55-70. Philadelphia: Temple University Press.

JANSSEN, PETER A.
July 4, 1970. "Education Vouchers." *The New Republic*.

JENCKS, CHRISTOPHER
Winter 1966. "Is the Public School Obsolete?" *The Public Interest*.

Nov. 3, 1968. "Private Schools for Black Children." *The New York Times Magazine*.

July 4, 1970. "Education Vouchers." *The New Republic*.

Sept. 1970. "Giving Parents Money for Schooling: Education Vouchers." *Phi Delta Kappan*. Pp. 49-52.

JENCKS, CHRISTOPHER, and DAVID REISMAN
1968. *The Academic Revolution.* Garden City, N.Y.: Doubleday & Co., Inc.

JENCKS, CHRISTOPHER, MARSHALL SMITH, HENRY ACLAND, et al.
1972. *Inequality.* New York: Basic Books Inc.

JENKINS, EVAN
Nov./Dec. 1973. "Stand By For Vouchers." *Compact.* Pp. 7-9

JEROME, JUDSON
1971. *Culture Out of Anarchy.* New York: Herder & Herder.

JOHNS, ROE L., IRVING J.GOFFMAN, KERN ALEXANDER, and DEWEY H.
    STOLLAR
1970. *Economic Factors Affecting the Financing of Education.* Vol. 2. Gainesville, Fla: National Education Finance Project.

JONES, PHILIP and SUSAN JONES
1976. *Parents Unite!* New York: Wyden Books.

KARIER, CLARENCE J.
1986 (1967). *The Individual, Society and Education, A History of American Educational Ideas.* 2d ed. Urbana, Ill.: University of Illinois Press.

KATZ, MICHAEL B.
Summer 1971. "From Voluntarism to Bureaucracy in American Education." *Sociology of Education.* Pp. 197-332.

KEARNS, DAVID T.
April 8, 1986. "Economics and the Student." *Vital Speeches of the Day.* (So. Carolina: City News Publisher). Pp. 563-67.

KELLEY, DAVID
Feb. 17, 1986. "Learning the Hard Way." *Barrons.* P. 11.

KERBER, AUGUST
1968. *Quotable Quotes on Education.* Detroit, Mich.: Wayne State University Press.

KIESLING, HERBERT J.
June 1975. *Educational Productivity: Public Concern and Legislative Response,* Washington, D.C.: National Conference of State Legislators, Legislators' Education Action Project.

KILPATRICK, JAMES. J.
May 7, 1970. "School Tuition Scheme." Harrisburg, Pa.: *The Patriot.*

Nov. 23, 1970. "Accountability in the Schoolhouse." Allentown, Pa.: *Morning Call.*

March 25, 1986. "Voucher Plan gives poor access to better education." Harrisburg, Pa.: *The Evening News.*

KIRKPATRICK, DAVID W.
May 1970. "The President's Message." Harrisburg, Pa.: *Pennsylvania School Journal.* P. 234.

Sept. 1970. "The Agony of Relevance." Harrisburg, Pa.: *Pennsylvania School Journal.* Pp. 71-74.

April 1971. "What Is the Future in Education for Teachers?" Harrisburg, Pa.: *Pennsylvania School Journal.* Pp. 254-56.

March/April, 1988. "Tuition Vouchers." *Home Education.* Pp. 17-19.

KIRP, DAVID L., and MARK G.YUDOF
1974. *Educational Policy and the Law.* Berkeley, Calif.: McCutchan Publishing Corp.

KIRST, MICHAEL, and JAMES CATERALL
April 1980. "Voucher and Jarvis II in California—Out of the Pan Into the Fire." In *IFG Policy Notes 1.* (Palo Alto, Calif.)

KOERNER, JAMES D.
Jan. 1, 1974. "Changing Education, The Gullibility of Teachers and Administrators." *Vital Speeches of the Day.* (So. Carolina: City News Publisher). Pp. 177-81.

KOHL, HERBERT
    1967. *36 Children.* New York: The New American Library.

    1969. *The Open Classroom.* New York: The New York Review.

KOZOL, JONATHAN
    1967. *Death at an Early Age.* Boston: Houghton Mifflin.

    1978. *Children of the Revolution.* New York: Delacorte.

KRUGHOFF, ROBERT M.
    Nov. 1969. "Private Schools for the Public," *Education and Urban Society.*

KUTNER, MARK A., JOEL D. SHERMAN, and MARY F. WILLIAMS
    1986. "Federal Policies for Private Schools." In *Private Education.* Ed. Daniel C. Levy. Pp. 57-81. New York: Oxford University Press.

LAMM, RICHARD
    Nov. 1986. "Can Parents Be Partners?" *Phi Delta Kappan.* Pp. 211-13.

LANOUE, GEORGE R., ED.
    1972. *Educational Vouchers: Concepts and Controversies.* New York: Columbia Univ. Teachers College Press.

LAZERSON, MARVIN, JUDITH BLACK MCLAUGHLIN, BRUCE MCPHERSON, and STEPHEN K. BAILEY
    1985. *An Education of Value.* Cambridge, England: Cambridge University Press.

LEACOCK, ELEANOR BURKE
    1969. *Teaching and Learning in City Schools.* New York: Basic Books Inc.

LEGISLATIVE JOURNAL-SENATE.
    June 2, 1975. Harrisburg, Pa: Commonwealth of Pa.

LEGISLATIVE REVIEW
    Oct. 6, 1975. Denver, Colo.: Education Commission of the States.

LESSINGER, LEON
 1970. *Every Kid a Winner.* New York: Simon & Schuster.

LEVIN, HENRY M.
 n.d. (1969?). *The Failure of the Public Schools and the Free Market Remedy.* Wichita, Kansas: Center for Independent Education of Wichita Collegiate School.

 1969. *Community Control of Schools.* Washington, D.C.: Brookings Institution.

 October 1973. "Vouchers and Social Equity." *Change Magazine.* Pp. 29-33.

 1975. "Educational Vouchers and Educational Quality." In *Schooling in a Corporate Society.* Ed. Martin Carnoy. New York: David McKay.

 1980. "Educational Vouchers and Social Policy." In *School Finance Policies and Practices —The 1980s: A Decade of Conflict* Ed. James W. Guthrie. Pp. 235-63. Cambridge, Mass.: Ballinger Publishing Co.

 July 1982. *Educational Choice and the Pains of Democracy.* Stanford University, Calif.: Institute for Research on Educational Finance and Governance. Prepared for the Tuition Tax Credit Seminar, Wash., D.C. Document sponsored by NIE, Wash. D.C., Report No. 1FG-TCC-11.

LEVIN, HENRY M.
 1983. "Educational Choice and the Pains of Democracy." In *Public Dollars for Private Schools.* Ed. Thomas James and Henry M. Levin. Pp. 17-38. Philadelphia: Temple University Press.

LEVIN, JOEL M.
 Summer (1973?). *Final Report on First Year Operations of the Alum Rock Voucher Project.* Prepared by the Sequoia Institute.

 November 1974. "Alum Rock After Two Years." *Phi Delta Kappan.* Pp. 201-204.

LEVY, DANIEL C.
1986. "'Private' and 'Public': Analysis Amid Ambiguity in
Higher Education." In *Private Education*. Ed. Daniel C. Levy.
Pp. 170-192. NY: Oxford University Press.

LEWIS, ANNE C.
January 1986. "Washington Report." *Phi Delta Kappan*. P. 331.

LIEBERMAN, MYRON
Feb. 17, 1986. "Why School Reform Isn't Working." *Fortune*.
Pp. 135-36.

June 1986. "Privatization and Public Education." *Phi Delta
Kappan*. Pp. 731-34.

1986. *Beyond Public Education*. New York: Praeger.

LIFE MAGAZINE
March 24, 1958. "Crisis in Education." (Part 1 of a 5-part
weekly series).

LIGHTFOOT, SARA LAWRENCE
1978. *Worlds Apart: Relationships Between Families and Schools*.
NY: Basic Books.

LISTER, IAN
1974. *Deschooling*. Cambridge, England: Cambridge University
Press.

LOFTON, JOHN D.
July 15, 1974. Lancaster, Pa.: *The New Era*.

LONDON, HERBERT I.
May/June 1987. "Death of the University." *The Futurist*. Pp.
17-22.

LOTT, JOHN R., JR.
June 26, 1986. Harrisburg, Pa.: *The Patriot*. P. A13.

LYON, DAVID W.
December 1971. "Capitalism in the Classroom: Education
Vouchers." *Business Review*. Federal Reserve Bank of
Philadelphia.

LYTLE, R. J.
    1975. *Liberty Schools.* Farmington, Mich.: Structures Publishing
    Co.

MACCHIAROLA, FRANK, and THOMAS HAUSER
    1985. *For Our Children: A Different Approach to Public Education.*
    New York: Continuum.

MADDOX, GEORGE L.
    May 1974. *Adults as Learners.* University Park, Pa.: Penn State
    University.

MARBURGER, CARL
    1985. *One School at a Time.* Columbia, Md.: The National
    Committee for Citizens in Education.

MARIN, PETER
    Sept. 19, 1970. "Children of the Apocalypse." *Saturday Review.*

MARTIN, JOHN HENRY, and CHARLES H. HARRISON
    1972. *Free To Learn.* Englewood Cliffs, N.J.: Prentice-Hall, Inc.

MATTFELD, JACQUELYN ANDERSON.
    Fall 1974. "Liberal Education in Contemporary American
    Society." *Daedulus.* Pp. 282-87.

MAZZONI, TIM, and BARRY SULLIVAN
    1986. "State Government and Educational Reform in Minne-
    sota." In *The Fiscal, Legal and Political Aspects of State Reform of
    Elementary and Secondary Education.* Ed. Van D. Mueller and
    Mary P. McKeown. Pp. 169-202. Cambridge, Mass.: Ballinger
    Publishing Co.

McCANN, WALTER
    Summer 1972. "The Politics and Ironies of Educational
    Change—The Case of Vouchers." *Yale Review of Law and Social
    Action.* Pp. 374-89.

McCARTHY, TIMOTHY S.
    Fall 1975. "A Matter of Choice." *Information NIE* (Quarterly
    Journal of the National Institute of Education). P. 607.

McGuire, Kent
　　1986. "Implications for Future Reform: A State Perspective."
　　In *The Fiscal, Legal, and Political Aspects of State Reform of
　　Elementary and Secondary Educatio.* Ed. Van D. Mueller and
　　Mary P. McKeown. Pp. 309-24. Cambridge, Mass.: Ballinger
　　Publishing Co.

Mead, Margaret
　　June 1971. "Are Any School Administrators Listening?"
　　Nation's Schools. Pp. 41-45.

Melton, David
　　1975. *Burn The Schools—Save The Children.* New York: Thomas
　　Y. Crowell.

Michaelson, Jacob B.
　　1980. "Efficiency, Equity, and the Need for a New Educational
　　Policy." In *School Finance Policies and Practices—The 1980s: A
　　Decade of Conflict.* Ed. James W. Guthrie. Pp. 207-33.
　　Cambridge, Mass.: Ballinger Publishing Co.

Mill, John Stuart
　　1966 (1912). *On Liberty, Representative Government, The Subjec-
　　tion of Women (Three Essays).* London: Oxford Univ. Press;
　　original pub. 1859.

Millett, John D.
　　July 30, 1975. "Creative Management in a Time of Economic
　　Decline." A paper presented at a seminar of the State Higher
　　Education Executive Officers Association, New Orleans, La.

Moynihan, Sen. Daniel Patrick
　　1981. "What the Congress Can Do When the Court Is Wrong."
　　In *Private Schools and the Public Good.* Ed. Edward McGlynn
　　Gaffney, Jr. Pp. 79-84. Notre Dame, Indiana: University of
　　Notre Dame Press.

Mueller, Van D., and Mary P. McKeown
　　1985. *The Fiscal, Legal and Political Aspects of State Reform of
　　Elementary and Secondary Education.* Cambridge, Mass.: Ballin-
　　ger Publishing Co.

MURNANE, RICHARD J.

1983. "The Uncertain Consequences of Tuition Tax Credits: An Analysis of Student Achievement and Economic Incentives." In *Public Dollars for Private Schools*. Ed. Thomas James and Henry M. Levin. Pp. 210-22. Philadelphia: Temple University Press.

1986. "Comparisons of Private and Public Schools: The Critical Role of Regulations." In *Private Education*. Ed. Daniel C. Levy. Pp. 138-52. New York: Oxford University Press.

NAKAO, ANNIE

July 1979. "The Coons-Sugarman Initiative Campaign to Revolutionize the California Schools Through Vouchers." *California Journal*. Pp. 237-39.

NATHAN, JOE

1983. *Free To Teach*. New York: The Pilgrim Press.

March 1985. "The Rhetoric and the Reality of Expanding Educational Choices." *Phi Delta Kappan*. Pp. 476-81.

THE NATION

June 29, 1970. "No Magic in Vouchers." P. 773.

NATIONAL COMMISSION ON EXCELLENCE IN EDUCATION

1983. *A Nation at Risk: The Imperative for Educational Reform*. Washington, D.C.: Government Printing Office.

NATIONAL EDUCATION ASSOCIATION CONVENTION PROCEEDINGS

1968.

THE NATIONAL ELEMENTARY PRINCIPAL

January 1971. Opinion Poll. Pp. 98-99.

THE NATIONAL GOVERNORS' ASSN.

June 24, 1987. *Time for Results, The Governors' 1991 Report on Education*. Quoted in *Education Week*. P. C3.

THE NATIONAL OBSERVER

Feb. 2, 1970. "Parents Would Buy Schooling With a Voucher."

NATION'S SCHOOLS
> January 1971. Opinion Poll. "Reactions to vouchers: hostility, scepticism." P. 89.

> February 1971. Report from Washington. "OEO reported ready to announce test sites for voucher plan." P. 11.

NEA Today
> April 1, 1986. Opinion Poll. P. 13.

NEWMAN, FRANK
> 1973. *The Second Newman Report: National Policy and Higher Education.* Cambridge, Mass.: The MIT Press.

> 1985. *Higher Education and the American Resurgence.* Princeton, N.J.: The Carnegie Foundation for the Advancement of Teaching.

NEWSWEEK
> Aug. 10, 1970. "Pay-as-You-Go Schooling." P. 49.

> April 26, 1976. "The Middle-Class Pinch." P. 63.

> Jan. 26, 1987. "Perspectives." Page of selected quotes. P. 19.

> Oct. 26, 1987. "Inching Toward More School." Pp. 75-76.

> May 16, 1988. "Voters like vouchers." P. 8.

NYQUIST, EWALD B.
> Dec. 15, 1973. "Non-Traditional Studies." *Vital Speeches of the Day.* (So. Carolina: City News Publisher). Pp. 154-59.

O'DONNELL, MARGARET G.
> 1985. *The Educational Thought of the Classical Political Economists.* Lanham, Md.: University Press of America.

ORNSTEIN, ALLAN C.
> February 1971. "Decentralizing Urban Schools." *Journal of Secondary Education.* Pp. 83-91.

PAINE, THOMAS
> 1969. "The Rights of Man, Part Second." In *The Complete Writing of Thomas Paine.* Ed. Philip S. Foner. New York: The Citadel Press, 2 vols. (1st ed., London, February 1792).

PAINTER, KIM
> October 1, 1986. "Public Schools can learn from private schools." *USA Today.* P. D1.

PARKER, FRANKLIN
> September 1978. "Intriguing Finance Reform Ideas for the Salvation of U.S. Public Schooling." Review of *School Finance* by Walter I. Garms, James W. Guthrie, and Lawrence C. Pierce. In *Phi Delta Kappan.* P. 68.

PASSOW, A. HARRY
> 1976. *Secondary Education Reform: Retrospect and Prospect.* New York: Teachers College Press, Columbia University.

THE PATRIOT (Harrisburg, Pa.)
> Dec. 16, 1986. "Fundamentalists Get Award for Schooling Costs." P. A1.

> Dec. 30, 1986. "Vouchers proposed for remedial classes." P. A4.

PEARSON, GEORGE E.
> n.d. (1971?). *Another Look at Education Vouchers.* Wichita, Kansas: Center for Independent Education.

PEIRCE, NEAL
> Nov. 8, 1986. "Grade Many School Boards with an F." *The Philadelphia Inquirer.* P. A11.

PENNSYLVANIA SCHOOL BOARDS ASSN.
> Sept./Oct. 1976. "12 major events that shaped American education." *PSBA BULLETIN.* Harrisburg, Pa.

PENNSYLVANIA STATE EDUCATION ASSN.
> Oct. 6, 1969. *The Voice of PSEA.* Harrisburg, Pa.: Pa. State Education Assn.

PENNSYLVANIA STATE EDUCATION ASSN. (cont.)
April 6, 1970. *President's Notes*, p. 1.. Harrisburg, Pa: Pa. State Education Assn.

1976. *PSEA Bicentennial Symposium on Education.* Harrisburg, Pa.: Pa. State Education Assn.

PHI DELTA KAPPAN
May 1971. Editorial page. P. 512.

May 1971. "Vouchers have been rejected . . ." P. 568.

September 1973. "Voucher Experiment Assessment." P. 77.

March 1983. "Decade after Rodriguez: An Interview with John Coons." Pp. 479-80.

PIPHO, CHRIS
March 1985. "Student Choice: The Return of the Voucher." *Phi Delta Kappan*. P. 461.

POSTMAN, NEIL, and CHARLES WEINGARTNER
1969. *Teaching as a Subversive Activity.* New York: Delacorte Press.

1973. *The School Book.* New York: Delacorte Press.

PRATTE, RICHARD
1973. *The Public School Movement.* New York: David McKay Co. Inc.

PTA MAGAZINE
Nov. 1970. "PTA Opposes OEO Voucher System." Pp. 30-31.

RAVITCH, DIANE
1985. *The Schools We Deserve.* New York: Basic Books Inc.

RAYWID, MARY ANNE
June 1983. "Schools of Choice: Their Current Nature and Prospects." In *Phi Delta Kappan*. Pp. 684-88.

REED, SALLY D.
Jan. 28, 1986. "Educational Vouchers—Creating Parental Control." Greensburg, Pa.: *The Tribune-Review.*

REIMER, EVERETT
1971. *An Essay on Alternatives in Education.* Cuernavaca, Mexico: Centro Intercultural de Documentación.

REINHOLD, ROBERT
June 4, 1975. "School Vouchers: 'Quick Death' Raises Query on Validity of Test." New York: *The New York Times* .

THE REPORT OF THE WHITE HOUSE CONFERENCE ON YOUTH
April 18-22, 1971. Washington, D.C.: U.S. Government Printing Office.

RIBICOFF, SEN. ABRAHAM, A.
Feb. 23, 1970. Easton, Pa.: *The Express* Newspaper.

RICHARDSON, ANN
1977. *Vouchered Skill Training in WIN: Program Guidelines and elected Empirical Findings.* Wash. D.C.: Bureau of Social Science Research.

RICHBURG, KEITH
Nov. 10, 1985. "Reagan to urge education vouchers." Allentown, Pa.: *The Morning Call* Newspaper. P. A26.

ROGERS, CARL R.
1969. *Freedom to Learn.* Columbus, Ohio: Charles E. Merrill Publishing Co.

ROGERS, CORNISH
Oct. 7, 1970. "Jencks Education Plan: Sure to Backfire; National Education Voucher Plan." *Christian Century.* Pp. 1176-77.

ROGERS, DAVID
1968. *110 Livingston Street.* New York: Random House.

ROTHMAN, ROBERT
May 20, 1987. "Wilson Unveils Proposals to Reform Boston Schools." *Education Week.* P. 8.

SALGANIK, LAURA HERSH
March 1981. *The Fall and Rise of Educational Vouchers*, 44pp.
Wash. D.C.: NIE Report No. CS0S-R-307. Baltimore, Md.: Johns
Hopkins University. Center for Social Organization of Schools.

SANDOW, STUART, AND WESLEY APKER, EDS.
1975. *The Politics of Education: Challenges to State Board Leadership.* Bloomington, Ind.: Phi Delta Kappa Inc.

SAXE, RICHARD W.
1967. *Schools Don't Change.* New York: Philosophical Library
Inc.

SCALIA, ANTONIN
1978. *Testimony of the Constitutionality of Tuition Tax Credits.*
Washington, D.C.: American Enterprise Institute

1981. "On Making It Look Easy by Doing It Wrong." In *Private
Schools and the Public Good.* Ed. Edward McGlynn Gaffney, Jr.
Pp. 173-85. Notre Dame, Indiana: University of Notre Dame
Press.

SCHERER, JOSEPH J., and JIM STINSON
March 1985. "Voucher Debate Could Be Rekindled in 1985."
The School Administrator. Pp. 29-30.

SCHOOLBOYS OF BARBIANA
1970. *Letter to a Teacher.* New York: Random House.

SCHRAG, PETER
Sept. 19, 1970. "End of the Impossible Dream." *Saturday
Review.*

SCHUCHAT, THEODOR
April 1971. "With Education in Washington." *The Education
Digest*, 55-58.

SCHWARZ, ALAN
Unpublished. *Validity of a School Voucher Plan as Against an
Attack Under the Establishment Clause.* Prepared for Frank
Overlan, Director, Center for the Study of Public Policy,
Cambridge, Mass., 29 pp.

SELDEN, DAVID
June 1975. "Vouchers: A Critic Changes His Mind." *Nation's Schools and Colleges.* Pp. 44-46.

SHANKER, ALBERT
Fall 1986. "Our Profession, Our Schools: The Case for Fundamental Reforms." *American Education.*

SHERMAN, JOEL D.
1983. "Public Finance of Private Schools: Observations from Abroad." In *Public Dollars for Private Schools.* Pp. 71-83. Ed. Thomas James and Henry M. Levin. Phila.: Temple University Press.

SILBERMAN, CHARLES E.
1970. *Crisis in the Classroom.* New York: Random House.

SIZER, THEODORE E.
1984. *Horace's Compromise: The Dilemma of the American High School.* New York: Houghton Mifflin.

SIZER, THEODORE R., and RYLAND SIZER
Sept. 1976. "Education and Assimilation: A Fresh Plea for Pluralism." *Phi Delta Kappan.*

SIZER, THEODORE R., and PHILLIP WHITTEN
August 1968. "A Proposal for a Poor Children's Bill of Rights." *Psychology Today.* Pp. 59-63.

SMITH, ADAM
1966. *An Inquiry into the Nature and Causes of the Wealth of Nations.* 1st ed. London: W. Strahan and T. Cadell, 1776. Vol. I, 510 pp. Vol. II, 587 pp. (New York: August M. Kelley, Facsimile Edition—650 copies printed.)

SNIDER, WILLIAM
April 1, 1987. "Allow Parents to Choose Schools, Boston Task Force Recommends." *Education Week.* P. 9.

June 24, 1987. "The Call for Choice: Competition in the Marketplace." *Education Week.* Pp. C1-C5.

SNIDER, WILLIAM (cont.)
> May 4, 1988. "Minnesota Backs Nation's First Choice System. *Education Week*. Pp. 1, 13.

SNYDER, K. ALAN
> 1985. "Public and Private Schools." In *A New Agenda for Education*. Ed. Eileen M. Gardner. Washington, D.C.: The Heritage Foundation. Pp. 13-26.

SOWELL, THOMAS
> 1972. *Black Education, Myths and Tragedies*. New York: David McKay Co. Inc.

> Aug. 8, 1976. "A Black 'Conservative' Dissent." New York: *The New York Times Magazine*.

> 1977. "Choice in Education and Parent Responsibility." *Parents, Teachers, and Children*. San Francisco: Institute for Contemporary Studies.

> 1986. *Education: Assumptions Versus History*. Stanford, Calif.: Stanford University, Hoover Institution Press.

STROUFE, GERALD, E.
> Winter 1971. "Review of Education Vouchers" (The Jencks Report). *Educational Administration Quarterly*.

STURM, JOHN E., and JOHN E. PALMER
> 1971. *Democratic Legacy in Transition: Perspectives on American Education*. New York: Van Nostrand Reinhold.

SULLIVAN, DANIEL J.
> 1974. *Public Aid to Nonpublic Schools*. Lexington, Mass.: Lexington Books.

SULLIVAN, NEAL V.
> 1971. *Walk, Run, or Retreat: The Modern School Administrator*. Bloomington, Ind.: Indiana University Press.

SZANTO, HUBERT
> September 1978. "California Voucher Plan: A Private School Principal's Critique." *NASSP Bulletin*. Pp. 93-98.

TODAY'S EDUCATION
November 1970. "Vouchers Plan: NEA Position." P. 80.

TOFFLER, ALVIN
March 11, 1986. *USA Today*. P. B4.

TOPE, DONALD E., et al.
1965. *The Social Sciences View School Administration*. Englewood Cliffs, N.J.: Prentice-Hall.

TREESH, FREDERICK H.
July 7, 1970. "Voucher System May Alter American Public Education." Easton, Pa.: *The Express Newspaper*.

TYACK, DAVID, MICHAEL KIRST, and ELIZABETH HANSOT
Spring 1980. "Education Reform: Retrospect and Prospect." New York: Columbia University Teachers College Press. Pp. 253-69.

UMANS, SHELLY
1970. *The Management of Education*. Garden City, New York: Doubleday & Co. Inc.

U.S. NEWS AND WORLD REPORT
March 16, 1970, "Better Way To Spend the Education Dollar." P. 46.

Sept. 6, 1976. "Diluting the GI Bill of Rights. P. 69.

U.S. SUPREME COURT
1907. *Interstate Consolidated Street Railway Co. v. Mass.* 207 U.S. 79.

1908. *Quick Bear v. Leupp.* 210 U.S. 50.

1923. *Meyer v. Nebraska.* 262 U.S. 390.

1925. *Pierce v. Society of Sisters.* 268 U.S. 510.

1927. *Farrington v. Tokushige.* 273 U.S. 284.

1930. *Cochran v. La. Bd. of Ed.* 281 U.S. 370.

U.S. SUPREME COURT (cont.)

1943. *W. Va. Bd. of Ed. v. Barnette*. 319 U.S. 624.

1947. *Everson v. Bd. of Ed.* 330 U.S. 1.

1954. *Brown v. Bd. of Ed.* 347 U.S. 483.

1958. *Cooper v. Aaron.* 358 U.S. 1.

1962. *Engel v. Vitale.* 370 U.S. 421.

1963. *Abington v. Schemp.* 374 U.S. 203.

1968. *Allen v. Bd. of Ed.* 392 U.S. 236.

1970. *Walz v. Tax Commission.* 397 U.S. 664.

1971. *Griggs v. Duke Power.* 401 U.S. 424.

1971. *Lemon v. Kurtzman.* 403 U.S. 602.

1971. *Tilton v. Richardson.* 403 U.S. 672.

1972. *Wisconsin v. Yoder.* 406 U.S. 208.

1973. *Rodriguez v. San Antonio.* 411 U.S. 1.

1973. *Norwood v. Harrison.* 413 U.S. 455.

1973. *Committee for Public Education v. Nyquist.* 413 U.S. 756.

1973. *Sloan v. Lemon.* 413 U.S. 825.

1975. *Wood v. Strickland.* 420 U.S. 308.

1975. *Meek v. Pittenger.* 421 U.S. 349.

1976. *Runyon v. McCrary.* 427 U.S. 160.

1977. *Wolman v. Walter.* 433 U.S. 229.

1983. *Mueller v. Allen.* 463 U.S. 388.

U.S. SUPREME COURT (cont.)
  1986. *Witters v. Washington Dept. of Service for the Blind,* 54 LW 4135 (*The United States Law Week,* Jan. 28, 1986. Vol. 54, No. 29).

USA TODAY
  Dec. 11, 1985. "How do you feel about school vouchers?" Opinion Poll. P. A10.

UZZELL, LAWRENCE A.
  Jan. 4, 1985. "Contradictions of Centralized Education." In *The Wall Street Journal.* P. 14.

VERMILYE, DYCKMAN W., ED.
  1976. *Individualizing the System: Current Issues in Higher Education.* San Francisco: Jossey-Bass.

THE WALL STREET JOURNAL
  Aug. 28, 1986. "Governors Opt For Choice of Schools."

WASHBURN, S. L.
  Fall 1974. "Evolution and Education." *Daedulus.* Pp. 221-28.

WASSERMAN, MIRIAM
  1970. *The School Fix, NYC, USA.* New York: Outerbridge & Distenfrey.

WAUGH, WILLIAM T.
  April 10, 1971."School Vouchers Would Give Parents Dollar Power." Easton, Pa.: *The Express.*

WEILER, DANIEL, et al.
  June 1974. *A Public School Vouchers Demonstration; The First Year at Alum Rock.* Santa Monica, CA: The Rand Corporation.

WEINTRAUB, FREDERICK J.
  1981. "Nonpublic Schools and the Education of the Handicapped." In *Private Schools and the Public Good.* Ed. Edward McGlynn Gaffney, Jr. Pp. 49-55. Notre Dame, Ind.: University of Notre Dame Press.

WEST, E. G.
   1965. *Education and the State.* London: Institute of Economic Affairs.

   1970. *Education and the State.* London: Institute of Economic Affairs, 2d ed.

   November 1977. "The Perils of Public Education." In *The Freeman.* Pp. 681-99.

WHELAN, CHARLES M.
   March 17, 1974. "Voucher Programs and Church-Related Schools: Constitutional Considerations." A Memorandum Prepared at the request of the Center for the Study of Public Policy, Cambridge, Mass.

WILSON, JOHN W. and VICKY CAHAN
   Jan. 13, 1986. "Don't Expect any Miracles at the Hospitals." In *Business Week.* P. 98.

WISHARD, WILLIAM VAN DUSEN
   May/June 1987. "The 21st Century Economy." In *The Futurist.* Pp. 23-28.

WOLFF, ROBERT PAUL
   1969. *The Ideal of the University.* Boston: Beacon Press.

WOODRING, PAUL AND CASS, JAMES, EDS.
   1970. *Education in America, 1960-1969.* New York: Arno Press, 4 Vols. The monthly education supplements of *The Saturday Review.*

Index